Women and Horses

BROUGHT TO YOU BY

The books created by Equine Heritage Institute are designed to preserve the history and majesty of the horse. Our goal is to find, understand, and pass on the valuable data about equine use and its influence on humanity. The Equine Heritage Institute is a not for profit 503(c) and 100% of all proceeds from the sale of books, services, and products support Equine Heritage Institute's mission.

To make a donation to EHI, please visit www.ehi-donations.com

SPECIAL THANKS TO OUR TEAM

Mary Chris Foxworthy, Research Writer

Mary Chris Foxworthy's grandfather owned one of the last creameries in the United States that still used horse-drawn milk wagons; thus began a life-long love affair with horses. After graduating from college with a degree in Food Science and Communications, Mary Chris bought her first horse with her first paycheck. After graduation she worked in Marketing and Finance in the corporate world. During that time, she volunteered her Marketing and Fundraising skills for various non-profits and finally in 2006 left the corporate world to work in the area of Advancement until her retirement in 2016. She has served on the board of various equine associations and held a judge's card in Carriage Driving. She has published and presented numerous equine educational programs, written for several equine publications and won an award from American Horse Publications for one of her articles. Mary Chris is an active exhibitor in Carriage Driving and Dressage. Along with her husband, she enjoys spending time with their horses (three Morgans and a PRE), a bouncing Bearded Collie and two adult children."

Mary Chris Foxworthy on Tommy, one of her grandfather's milk wagon horses.

Abby David, Graphic Designer

Abby David's family has roots in the Walking Horse tradition and she grew up hearing tales of Ole Tobe the mule's antics, holiday wagon decorations, and trick riding. In her teens she spent her summers boarding the neighbors horses and playing at barrel racing in the back paddock with Thunder (pictured). She landed a job as a Graphic Designer at The Arts Center of Cannon County in 2004 and has worked in the print and digital mass communications industry continuously. Since marrying into a family in the racehorse business, she has enjoyed exploring a whole new world of horses and wearing big fancy hats. She also enjoys dancing in all it's forms and teaches in her local community.

Gloria Austin's Collection of Books

www.GloriaAustin.com

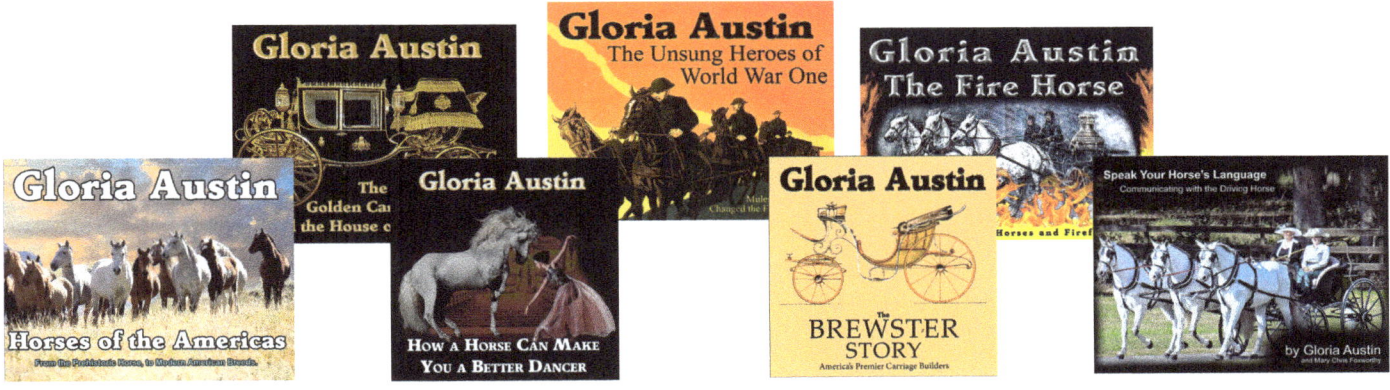

ENJOY OUR OTHER BOOKS

- How a Horse Can Make You a Better Dancer
- The Brewster Story
- Carriage Lamps
- Gloria Austin's Carriage Collection
- A Glossary of Harness Parts
- Equine Elegance
- The Fire Horse
- Horse Basics 101
- The Unsung Heros of World War One
- The Horse, History, and Human Culture
- Horse Symbolism
- Horses of the Americas
- A Drive Through Time: Carriages, Horses, and History
- Speak Your Horse's Language
- Tea: Steeped in Tradition
- The Golden Carriage and the House of Hapsburg

Brought To You By The Equine Heritage Institute

Women and Horses
By: Gloria Austin - President of Equine Heritage Institute, Inc. (EHI)

First Publish Date 2019
Copyright © 2019 by Equine Heritage Institute, Inc.

All rights reserved. No part of this publication may be reproduced, distributed, or transmitted in any form or by any means, including photocopying, recording, or other electronic or mechanical methods, without the prior written permission of the publisher, except in the case of brief quotations embodied in critical reviews and certain other noncommercial uses permitted by copyright law. For permission requests, write to the publisher, addressed "Attention: Permissions Coordinator," at the address below.

Gloria Austin Carriage Collection, LLC; Equine Heritage Institute, Inc.
3024 Marion County Road Weirsdale, FL 32195 Office: (352) 753-2826 Fax: (352) 753-6186

Ordering Information:
Quantity sales: Special discounts are available on quantity purchases by corporations, associations, and others. For details, contact the publisher at the address above.
Printed in the United States of America First Edition
Print - 978-1-951895-98-3, EBook - 978-1-951895-97-6

The Horse

"We have had 6,000 years of history with the domesticated horse and only 100 years with the automobile."

Gloria Austin

Table of Contents

Horse Crazy! 9
Warrior Women 10
    Zenobia 12
    Queen Boudica 14
    Tomoe Gozen 16
    Joan of Arc 17
    Nefertiti, Queen of the Nile 19
    Lozen 20
    Amazon Women 21
    Sybil Ludington 22
    Khutulun 23
    Gudit 24
    Mai Bhago 25
    The Gladiatrix 26
  Modern Day Warrior Woman Journaling Page 28
Queens 30
    Queen Laxmibai 32
    Queen Isabella of Spain 34
    Marie henrietta of Austria Queen of the Belgians 35
    Empress Elisabeth of Austria 35
    Catherine the Great 36
    Empress Augusta-Viktoria 37
    Princess Cecilie of mecklenbury-Schwerin Crown Princess of Germany and Prussia 37
    Queen Wilhelmina of the Netherlands 38
    Empress Alexandra of Russia 38
    Queen Victoria 39
    Queen Elizabeth I 41
    Queen Elizabeth II 42
  Queen for a Day Journaling Page 44
Deities and Mythology 46
    Eos (Greek) Aurora (Roman) 49
    Hera 50
    Diana 50
    Rhiannon 51
    Epona 51
    Arion 52
    Aife (Aiofe) 52
    Astarte 52
    Xatel Ekwa 53
    Gna 53
    Etain Echraide 53
    Sanjna 54
    Mari 54
    Sol 54
    Aine 55
    Niamh 55
    Penthesilea Queen of the Amazons 56
    The Valkyries 57
  Modern Day Goddess Journaling Page 58
Trendsetters and Reformers 60
    Lady Godiva 62
    The Long Riders 63
    Katherine Hepburn 64
    Elizabeth Taylor 64
    Inez Milholland 65
    Lady Seymour Dorothy Worsley 66
    Catherine "Skittles" Walters 67
    Alberta Claire, "The Girl from Wyoming" 67
    Coco Chanel 68
  Blazing Trails Journaling Page 70
Performers 72
    Prairie Rose Henderson 74
    Two Gun Nan Aspinwall 75
    Annie Oakley 76
    Sonora Webster Carver 78
    Theresa Renz 79

Table of Contents

    Dale Evans 80
    Tatiana Tchalabaeva 81
    Camilla Naprous 82
In the Limelight Journaling Page 84
Competitors 86
    Eleonora R. Sears 88
    Lis Hartel 89
    Sheila Varian 90
    Cheryl White 91
    Julie Krone 91
    Penny Chenery 92
    Lucille Mulhall 93
    Tillie Baldwin 93
    Melanie Smith 94
    Helen Crabtree 95
Winners Journaling Page 96
Coaching and Carriage Driving Women 98
    The ladies Four-in-Hand Driving Club 100
    Loula Long Combs 102
    Charley Parkhurst 104
    A. Sylvia Brocklebank 104
    Alla Polzunova 105
A Driving Force Journaling Page 106
Authors and Artists 108
    Anna Sewell 110
    Marguerite Henry 111
    Sallie Walrond 112
    Gloria Austin 113
    Jeanne Mellin Herrick 114
    Elizabeth Thompson (Lady Butler) 115
    Elyne Mitchell 116
    Patricia Leitch 118
    Lucy Kemp-Welch 119

    Belle Beach Bain 120
    Rosa Bonheur 121
    Leaving a Legacy Journaling Page 122
Caregivers 124
    Linda Tellington Jones 126
    Florence Kimball, DVM 127
    Mary Ida Yound 128
    Carol Harris 129
    Ruth "Bazy" Tankersley 130
    M. Phyllis lose 131
    Nurturing and Carring Journaling Page 132
An Amazing Woman _____ 134
Sources 140

Horse Crazy!

Many little girls grow up thinking about horses 24 -7. They read about horses, they watch movies about horses, they play with Breyer® horses and, if they are lucky enough, they even get to ride horses.

These horse crazy girls often grow up to become competent horse women. Ninety percent of horse owners in the United States today are women. Some are authors, some are trainers, some are accomplished equestrians and some are simply backyard enthusiasts. They often share their love of horses with the next generation of horse crazy little girls.

From Deities to Olympians, join us and meet some of the most iconic horse women throughout the ages. As we meet famous women through the ages, we'll also explore the special bond that women have with horses and gain an insight into how and why this bond develops.

Along the way, you may learn why you have a special bond with horses too and....you may even see yourself as a Warrior Woman or a Trendsetter!

When you finish the book, we have left some room for you to journal about your horse experience or write about a friend and then gift the book to them.

Gloria Austin's first horse, Duke.

Lady, a grade horse, was Gloria Austin's second horse which she used for pole bending, flag racing, and barrel racing. Lady was younger and far more agile than Duke.

Gloria Austin driving four to a coach

Warrior Women

AMAZON.

Wonder Woman, Super Girl and Cat Woman are all comic book super heroines who perform marvelous feats to save the world from evil forces. History, however, provides us with real-life heroines who truly performed amazing deeds. These heroines did not have comic book super powers. They had something even more valuable in their quests. They had horses!

Tomoe Gozen

Amazon Women

Zenobia

Zenobia was born in Palmyra, Syria sometime around 240 AD. Syria was at this time a Roman province.

According to the Arabic version of her story, told by Al-Tabari, she was placed in charge of the family flocks and shepherds when she was a young girl and thereby grew used to controlling large groups. Al-Tabari also claims that this is when she became adept at riding horses and learned the endurance and stamina that made her famous. She was married to Odaenathus, the king of the Palmyrene Empire, and she bore him a son named Vaballathus.

Palmyra served as a border between the Roman Empire and the Persian Empire. However, the Sassanid Persians had been causing a good deal of trouble for the Romans since they had access to Eastern trade borders in and out of Rome. In 260 AD, the Roman emperor Valerian attempted to march against the Sassanids but was defeated. Following his defeat, Odaenathus went to battle against the Persians and was successfully able to drive them out of Syria and across the Euphrates River. This act greatly benefited the Romans and served to strengthen ties between the two empires. The Romans made Odaenathus the governor of the Eastern part of the Roman Empire. Odaenathus later styled himself king of Palmyra. The glory days of Odaenathus didn't last long. In 267 AD, Odaenathus and his first son were both murdered by a relative named Maeonius. After his death, Zenobia's son, Vaballathus, inherited the throne. At the time of his father's death, Vaballathus was still a child, so Zenobia took control, ruling the Palmyrene Empire as regent.

Palmyra, Syria

The Roman Empire was undergoing its Imperial Crisis at this time. Internal conflicts prevented the Empire from maintaining control far beyond the borders of Rome. Bit by bit, guided by the wisdom of her counselors, Zenobia pushed separation from Rome. She conquered all of Syria and most of Anatolia (Turkey in modern times). She marched her troops into Egypt and seized Alexandria. By 270 AD, she had full control of Egypt and the wealth that came with it. Her empire seemed to be unstoppable. The open defiance of Roman rule by Zenobia was not unnoticed by Aurelian, the new emperor of Rome. The fact that a woman ruler had managed to do so was beyond the pale for the Roman emperor. So Aurelian struck back at Palmyra. He reclaimed Roman territories that had been taken by Zenobia.

What happened to Zenobia after that? Some stories had her committing suicide or dying in a hunger strike; others had her beheaded by the Romans or dying of illness. Yet another story, which has some confirmation based on an inscription in Rome, had Zenobia being married to a Roman senator and living with him in Tibur (Tivoli, Italy) and having children. Queen Zenobia has been remembered in artwork and literary and historical works for centuries, including in Chaucer's "Canterbury Tales". (cited from: https://allthatsinteresting.com/zenobia and https://www.warhistoryonline.com/instant-articles/zenobia-queen-who-defied-rome.html and https://www.thoughtco.com/queen-zenobia-biography-3528385 and http://howarddavidjohnson.com/legendary-women.htm}

Aurelian, emperor of Rome

Queen Boudica

At the time of the Roman conquest of southern Britain (43 AD), Queen Boudica ruled the Iceni tribe of East Anglia with her husband, King Prasutagus. The Roman Governor of Britain at that time was Suetonius Paulinus. After Prasutagus's death, his lands and household were plundered by the Roman officers and their slaves. Suetonius had Prasutagus' widow Boudica publicly flogged and her daughters were raped by Roman slaves. Not surprisingly, these outrages provoked the Iceni and they began to rebel against the Romans.

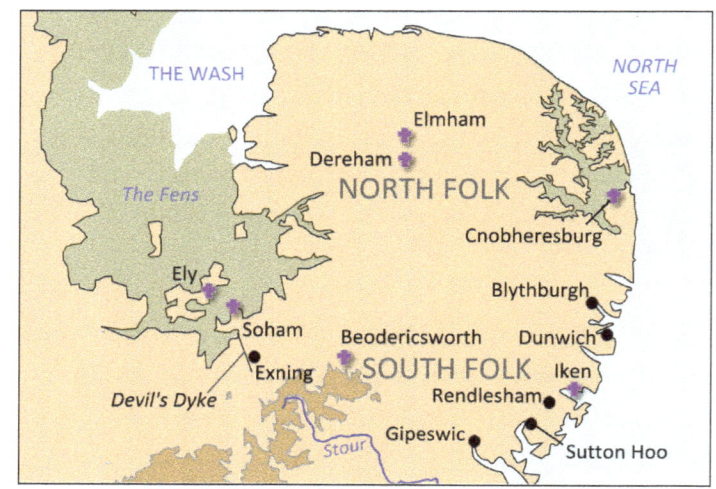

Boudica and her allies stormed Londinium (London) and Verulamium (St. Albans) and the defenders fled. The revolting Britons even desecrated the Roman cemeteries, mutilating statues and breaking tombstones. Some of these mutilated statues can be seen today in Colchester Museum.

Suetonius, who fled with his troops into relative safety of the Roman military zone, decided to challenge Boudica. He assembled an army of ten thousand men. Boudica and her daughters drove around in her chariot to all her tribes before the battle, exhorting them to be brave. She cried that she was descended from mighty men but she was fighting as an ordinary person for her people's lost freedom.

Statue mutilated by Roman soilders at Colchester Castle.

The Britons attacked, crowding in on the Roman defensive line. The order was given and a volley of several thousand heavy Roman javelins was thrown into the advancing Britons, followed quickly by a second volley. The lightly armed Britons must have suffered massive casualties within the first minutes of the battle. The Romans moved in for the kill, attacking in tight formation, stabbing with their short swords.

The Britons now had little chance. With so many of them involved in the battle, it is likely that their massed ranks worked against them by restricting their movements so that they were unable to use their long swords effectively. To ensure success, the Roman cavalry was released, which promptly encircled the enemy and began their slaughter from the rear. The Romans, seemingly mad with blood lust, killed eighty thousand men, women and children. The Roman losses amounted to four hundred dead with a slightly larger number wounded.

QUEEN BOADICEA LEADING THE BRITONS AGAINST THE ROMANS.

Boudica was not killed in the battle but took poison rather than be taken alive by the Romans. Boudica has secured a special place in British folk history, remembered for her courage as the Warrior Queen who fought the might of Rome. She was forgotten during the Middle Ages but then became legendary when Queen Victoria was seen as her namesake. In 1902, a bronze statue of her riding high in her chariot, designed by Thomas Thorneycroft, was placed on the Thames embankment next to the Houses of Parliament in the old Roman capital of Britain, Londinium. (cited from: https://www.historic-uk.com/HistoryUK/HistoryofEngland/Boudica/)

Tomoe Gozen

The legendary Japanese samurai are more often than not portrayed as men, but some of the country's most formidable warriors were a group of female samurai called the Onna-bugeisha. They used a special weapon called a naginata, that was designed specifically for women, that allowed them to have better balance because of their smaller stature. One of the most famous Onna-bugeisha was Tomoe Gozen. In the 12th century, there was no warrior that could match Tomoe Gozen's strength and agility.

Tomoe is only mentioned in an epic account of the late 12th century Genpei War known as, "The Tale of the Heike". Apart from this literary work, there are no other written records of Tomoe's life. In her appearance in "The Tale of Heike", Tomoe is portrayed as serving the samurai Minamoto Yoshinaka. Tomoe was already known as a warrior prior to the Battle of Awazu, which pitted Yoshinaka against one of his cousins, Minamoto Yoshitsune. The battle went badly for Yoshinaka, as he was heavily outnumbered by his enemy. Yoshinaka's army of three hundred strong was reduced by Yoshitsune (who had an army of six thousand), to just five warriors, Tomoe included. At this point, Yoshinaka ordered Tomoe to leave the battlefield, since he claimed that it would be shameful for him to die with a woman. Reluctantly, Tomoe obeyed Yoshinaka's command but not before beheading another of the enemy's warriors. After this, Tomoe disappeared from history and her fate has been speculated by various people.

In the "Genpei Seisuiki ", an extended version of "The Tale of the Heike", Tomoe is said to have been defeated by Wada Yoshimori and forced to become his concubine. In another story, she is said to have become a nun. In a third story, Tomoe is said to have avenged Yoshinaka by killing his enemies. After that, she took her lord's head and walked into the sea with it, thus ending her own life, and ensuring that Yoshinaka's head could not be defiled by his enemies.

No matter the end to the story, over the centuries, Tomoe has become quite an icon. (cited from: https://allthatsinteresting.com/women-warriors)

Joan of Arc

Joan of Arc (1412-1431), nicknamed "The Maid of Orléans", is considered a heroine of France for her role during the Lancastrian phase of the Hundred Years' War.

At the time of Joan of Arc's birth, France was embroiled in a long-running war with England known as the Hundred Years' War; the dispute began over who would be the heir to the French throne. By the early 15th century, northern France was a lawless frontier of marauding armies.

In 1415, King Henry V of England invaded northern France. After delivering a shattering defeat to French forces, England gained the support of the Burgundians in France. The 1420 Treaty of Troyes, granted the French throne to Henry V as regent for the insane King Charles VI. Henry would then inherit the throne after Charles' death. However, in 1422, both Henry and Charles died within a couple of months, leaving Henry's infant son as king of both realms. The French supporters of Charles' son, the future Charles VII, sensed an opportunity to return the crown to a French monarch. Around this time, Joan of Arc began to have mystical visions encouraging her to lead a pious life. Over time, the visions became more vivid, with the presence of St. Michael and St. Catherine designating her as the savior of France. The people in her visions encouraged her to seek an audience with Charles and ask his permission to expel the English and install Charles as the rightful king.

Joan cropped her hair and dressed in men's clothes for her eleven-day journey across enemy territory to Chinon, the site of Charles' court. Charles had prominent theologians examine her. The clergymen reported they found nothing improper with Joan, only piety, chastity and humility.

Charles gave the seventeen-year-old Joan of Arc armor and a horse and allowed her to accompany the army to Orléans, the site of an English siege. In a series of battles between May 4 and May 7, 1429, the

French troops took control of the English fortifications. Joan was wounded, but later returned to the front to encourage a final assault. By mid-June, the French had routed the English and, in doing so, their perceived invincibility as well. After the victory at Orléans, she kept encouraging Charles to hurry to Reims to be crowned king, but he and his advisors were more cautious. However, Charles and his procession finally entered Reims, and he was crowned Charles VII on July 18, 1429. Joan was at his side, occupying a visible place at the ceremonies.

In the spring of 1430, King Charles VII ordered Joan of Arc to Compiègne to confront the Burgundian assault. During the battle, she was thrown off her horse and left outside the town's gates. The Burgundians took her captive and held her for several months, negotiating with the English, who saw her as a valuable propaganda prize. Finally, the Burgundians exchanged Joan for ten thousand francs.

Charles was unsure what to do. Still not convinced of Joan's divine inspiration, he distanced himself and made no attempt to have her released. Though Joan's actions were against the English occupation army, she was turned over to church officials who insisted she be tried as a heretic. She was charged with seventy counts, including witchcraft, heresy and dressing like a man. On May 29, 1431, the tribunal announced Joan of Arc was guilty of heresy. On the morning of May 30, she was taken to the marketplace in Rouen and burned at the stake, before an estimated crowd of ten thousand people. She was nineteen years old.

After Joan's death, the Hundred Years' War continued for another twenty two years. Charles ultimately retained his crown and he ordered an investigation that in 1456 declared Joan of Arc to be officially innocent of all charges and designated a martyr. She was canonized as a saint on May 16, 1920. She is the patron saint of France. (cited from: https://www.biography.com/military-figure/joan-of-arc)

Nefertiti, Queen of the Nile

One of the most mysterious and powerful women in ancient Egypt was Nefertiti. Nefertiti was queen alongside Pharaoh Akhenaten from 1353 to 1336 BC. On the walls of tombs and temples, built during Akhenaten's reign, Nefertiti is shown alongside her husband more often than any other Egyptian queen. In many paintings she is shown in positions of power and authority driving a chariot.

New quartz head of Nefertiti, once believed to be the unisex pharaoh himself. Identified by Dr Christian E. Loeben, Egyptologist at the August Kestner Museum in Hanover, Germany.

Nefertiti's famous portrait is the polychrome bust found at Tell el-Amarna by German archaeologist Ludwig Borchardt in 1912 and kept in the Berlin Museum.

In this tomb painting in the tomb of Meryre, high priest of the Aten, Queen Nefertiti is shown smaller and follows the Pharaoh. Like him, she drives her chariot, drawn by a team of horses, whip in hand and without a driver.

During Akhenaten's reign (and perhaps after) Nefertiti enjoyed unprecedented power and by the twelfth year of Akhenaten's reign, there is evidence that she may have been elevated to the status of co-regent, equal in status to the pharaoh himself. (cited from: https://www.ancient-origins.net/history-famous-people/ten-powerful-and-fearsome-women-ancient-world-002947)

Lozen

Lozen is one of history's fiercest women warriors.

The name "Lozen" is an Apache war title, given to one who has stolen horses in a raid.

Apart from her prowess as a warrior, Lozen is reputed to have been a skilled military strategist as well as being highly proficient when it came to medicinal matters. Additionally, Lozen was her people's spiritual leader and, according to legend, possessed spiritual abilities that enabled her to detect the movement of her enemies.

By the age of twenty, Lozen was an expert at stealing horses. In addition, Lozen was skillful at riding, shooting and planning strategies. She fought alongside her brother, Victorio, and often sat beside him at council ceremonies as well as participating in warrior ceremonies. An often quoted saying by Victorio is that Lozen was his "right hand, strong as a man, braver than most, and cunning in strategy."

On the way to Florida, the Apache exiles stop briefly in Texas where this photo was taken. Lozen and Dahteste are seated together, top row. Geronimo and Chief Naiche are on bottom row.

In 1870 the Apache were driven out of their lands and onto reservations. Lozen and her people were on the San Carlos Reservation, where, in 1877 they decided to escape from its harsh conditions. They managed to make it back onto their own lands but had to fight to preserve their freedom. Two years later, they were sent onto another reservation. In 1880, Victorio was killed in a battle. Lozen and a small band of warriors wanted revenge and began raids across New Mexico and Arizona. Eventually, Lozen and her warriors joined forces with Geronimo. When Geronimo surrendered in 1886, his followers, including Lozen, were first sent to Florida and then to Alabama. The Apache were not used to the climate of their new home and many died of diseases such as diphtheria and tuberculosis. Lozen was one of these. She died in 1889 as a result of tuberculosis.
(cited from: https://www.ancient-origins.net/history-famous-people/lozen-intelligent-and-brave-apache-warrior-women-005889)

Amazon Women

The Scythians migrated from central Asia to southern Russia, centering over the present day Crimean peninsula, in the 8th and 7th centuries BC.

The tribe was artistic, violent and comprised entirely of excellent horse riders. They were among the earliest people to master horseback riding, a tactical advantage that astonished and overwhelmed their neighbors. Every Scythian had at least one personal mount, but the wealthy owned vast herds. Even the women rode. The Greek author Herodotus described the Scythian warrior women as "Amazon" women.

Herodotus reported that the Sarmatians were said to be the offspring of Scythians who had mated with Amazons and that their female descendants "have continued from that day to the present to observe their ancient Amazon customs, frequently hunting on horseback with their husbands; in war taking the field; and wearing the very same dress as the men." Moreover, said Herodotus, "No girl shall wed till she has killed a man in battle."

The story of the Amazons nearly went cold after Herodotus. Until, that is, the early 1990s when a joint U.S.-Russian team of archaeologists made an extraordinary discovery while excavating two thousand year old burial mounds outside Pokrovka, a remote Russian outpost in the southern Ural Steppes near the Kazakhstan border. There, they found over one hundred fifty graves belonging to the Sauromatians and their descendants, the Sarmatians. Among the burials of "ordinary women", the researchers uncovered evidence of women who were anything but ordinary. There were graves of warrior women who had been buried with their weapons. One young female, bowlegged from constant riding, lay with an iron dagger on her left side and a quiver containing forty bronze-tipped arrows on her right. The skeleton of another female still had a bent arrowhead embedded in the cavity. Nor was it merely the presence of wounds and daggers that amazed the archaeologists. On average, the weapon-bearing females measured five feet six inches, making them extraordinarily tall for their time. Finally, here was evidence of the women warriors that could have inspired the "Amazon" myths. In recent years, a combination of new archaeological finds, and a reappraisal of older discoveries, has confirmed that Pokrovka was no anomaly.

To the people of the time, the Scythian women must have seemed like incredible aberrations, ghastly even!(cited from: https://www.smithsonianmag.com/history/amazon-women-there-any-truth-behind-myth-180950188/)

Sybil Ludington

The American Revolution was a local war, with friends and families on opposite sides, spies next door and battles right in their neighborhoods. Everyday citizens knew what was at stake and aided the war effort in a multitude of ways. Sixteen year-old Sybil Ludington was one of these informal soldiers. Her father, Colonel Ludington, had trained his family on how to protect each other and their home.

When a messenger arrived at the Ludington farm on April 26, 1777, too exhausted to travel further, Sybil became the logical choice to ride out and muster the militia. Her father needed to stay at the farm and order the troops as they arrived.

British General William Tryon had landed off the coast, moving inland unopposed. His two thousand soldiers reached the town of Danbury, Connecticut and set fire to private homes and the Continental Army storehouses of meat, flour, rice, molasses, uniforms, shoes and gunpowder; all vital supplies for the colonists' war effort. The message that Danbury was burning was an important one. If Tryon's army continued, they would soon reach the large warehouses at Fredericksburg, potentially crippling the revolutionary movement or, they could attack General George Washington's army two days away at Peekskill.

The militia troops had taken a break from months of battle and had returned home to plant their spring crops and were scattered across many miles and they needed to learn this information. Sybil mounted up. She took off through the dark rain, riding from farm to farm on the forty-mile circuit. When she finally reached home at dawn, nearly four hundred militiamen had gathered on the Ludington farm. They immediately marched to Danbury, fewer in number than the British but with surprise on their side. The British may also have been hindered by consuming the colonists' stores of rum the night before. This became known as the Battle of Ridgefield. The militia joined with Continental Army troops to drive General Tryon's army back to their ships, an instrumental day in preserving the course of the American War of Independence. The militia were able to push the British off Long Island Sound thanks to Sybil's quick warning. (cited from: http://www.equitrekking.com/articles/entry/sybil-ludington-and-her-horse-star-heroes-of-the-american-revolution/)

Khutulun

Khutulun, (c.1260—c.1306 AD) was the daughter of the Mongolian leader, Kaidu, and the niece of Kublai Khan. By 1280 her father became the most powerful ruler of Central Asia. His territories stretched from the Central Siberian Plateau all the way to India.

Khutulun was described by many, including Marco Polo, as a superb warrior, horsewoman and wrestler. Being a Mongolian princess, she had many suitors. She told them that she would marry them if they could defeat her in wrestling. If they did not, they would have to surrender a few of their horses. Khutulun received nearly ten thousand horses by this means!

From 1260 to 1294, Khutulun assisted her father against Mongolian invaders, who wished to take her father's country. Because of her advice, willingness to help, and intelligence, Khutulun was the favorite child of Kaidu. It is reported that he tried to name her as his heir before he died in 1301, but this was rejected by male relatives who felt that they had the stronger claim. When he died, Khutulun, along with her brother, guarded her father's tomb against robbers and looters. She died in 1306.(cited from: https://badassladiesofhistory.wordpress.com/2014/06/09/khutulun/)

This miniature from a manuscript of the Livre des merveilles du monde, or The Travels of Marco Polo, depicts the Mongol princess Khutulun (c. 1260-1306) wrestling a suitor for her hand in marriage.

Gudit

The fall of the Aksumite kingdom of Ethiopia toward the end of the 10th century AD was attributed to a queen who invaded from the south. Though a subject of great mystery and differing opinions, most sources agree on one certainty; there existed an Ethiopian woman, who in the 10th century AD, led an army that attacked the Ethiopian state of Axum. She laid waste to the Christian churches and monuments in the region. In the process she devastated the countryside and hunted down and killed numerous members of the two thousand year old Solomonid dynasty. She massacred Christians and seized the throne for herself.

She is known by several different names, in varying texts, including Esther, Yodit, Judith and Esato. European, Arabic and African scholars still debate her mysterious life, origins and motives to this day.

The church of Abreha and Atsbeha in eastern Tigray in 1970, Bares an intricately carved ceiling blackened by soot. Priests will explain it as the work of Gudit, who had piled the church full of hay and set it ablaze nine centuries before.

Whatever her origins or real name, Gudit's conquering of Axum put an end to that nation-state's reign of power. Her attack came so swift and efficiently, that the Axumite forces were scattered in her army's wake. The Axumite king at the time sent a letter to the Patriarch of Alexandria, Egypt pleading for him to send whatever forces were possible from the Christian world to aid against an unknown warrior queen who rode at the head of a horse-backed army that was systematically decimating his kingdom. No help ever arrived. Gudit reigned for at least forty years, unchallenged. (cited from: http://www.africaspeaks.com/reasoning/index.php?topic=1103.0;wap2)

Mai Bhago

Mai Bhago, also known as Mata Bhag Kaur, was a Sikh woman who fought against the Mughal Empire in the early 18th century.

Mai Bhago was born in the village of Jhabal Kalan in the Punjab region of northern India. In addition to being taught Sikh traditions, she was trained by her father in horse riding and martial arts. She was a young woman during the period when oppression of Sikhs by the Mughal Empire was at its height. During 1704-05, the expansionist Mughal Emperor, Aurangzeb, invaded Sikh territory with an army of sixteen thousand troops and laid siege to the Sikh capital of Anandpur Sahib.

During the siege, the Sikh leader, Guru Gobind Singh Ji, was abandoned by forty of his elite warriors. Many of these men came from the region that Mai Bhago lived in and, according to some accounts, one of the deserters was her own husband. Outraged by this betrayal, Mai Bhago took her own horse, armor and weapons and left home to track down the deserters. She went to their homes and persuaded their wives not to give their husbands shelter. Some of the women even armed themselves and joined Mai Bhago, pledging to fight for the Guru if their husbands would not. Shamed by this, the forty deserters agreed to return to service with Mai Bhago.

During this time the Guru had escaped from the siege of Anandpur and was in retreat with his army. On December 29th, 1705, Mai Bhago's small force helped to cover the Guru's retreat at the Battle of Muktsar. Knowing that the pursuing Mughals would need water she set up camp at the Khidrana reservoir, erecting numerous empty tents and clothes lines to make it appear as if a larger army was encamped there. When the Mughal army attacked the empty tents, Mai Bhago's force ambushed them and, in spite of being heavily outnumbered, managed to push the Mughals back after intense fighting. Although victorious, Mai Bhago was the only Sikh survivor of the battle.

After the battle Mai Bhago joined up with the Guru's army and became his bodyguard. After the Guru's death in 1708 she retired to Jinvara, where she lived to an old age. Today she is remembered as a Sikh heroine whose actions served to ensure the survival of her faith. (cited from: http://thefemalesoldier.com/blog/mai-bhago)

The Gladiatrix

Female gladiators (gladiatrix) were just a thing of legend for many years. However, decades of research have made it possible to finally confirm their existence and importance in the Ancient Roman culture of gladiator fights.

The example of the 3rd century AD early Christian martyrs Perpetua and Felicitas being killed within the amphitheater at Carthage is just one example of the existence of women in the ancient Roman arena. Film and TV might lead the modern viewer to see women as passive parts of the Roman games, but in reality, both literary and archaeological examples attest to the use of trained female fighters within the arena.

The gladiatrix were usually wealthy Roman women who liked to fight and treated it as a form of entertainment and sport or believed it a way to find a special role in society. According to Tacitus (56-117AD), their exploits were hardly ever viewed by noble men, but at the same time, their fights were extremely popular. It was also said that the senators disgraced themselves if they watched the gladiatrix in the amphitheater. The women also didn't fight to

Both men and women wore jewelry, including brooches to hold their cloaks in place. Snake bracelets were popular, as well as gold necklaces set with precious stones. For women, a pale face was a status symbol. Poor women had rough, red faces from working outside. They used creams that contained flour, chalk, and lead to whiten their skin.

earn money, as they were already very rich. It has been argued that they were looking for attention, excitement and notoriety. All they needed to do to be a galdiatrix was to receive special permission from a person who arranged the fight.

Female gladiators probably appeared for the first time during the reign of Emperor Nero. The Roman historian, Cassius Dio, described the festival of gladiator fights, which was held as a tribute to Nero's mother, as follows: "In honor of his mother he (Nero) celebrated a most magnificent and costly festival, the events taking place for several days in five or six theaters at once. There was another exhibition that was at once most disgraceful and most shocking, when men and women not only of the equestrian but even of the senatorial order, appeared as performers in the orchestra, in the Circus, and in the hunting theatre, like those who are held in lowest esteem…; they drove horses, killed wild beasts and fought as gladiators, some willingly and some sore against their will."

The Ludus magnus in Rome: barracks for gladiators built by Emperor Domitian (81–96 CE), view from Via Labicana. In the background, the Colosseum.

Archaeological evidence has confirmed the existence of the women fighters that were described in ancient Roman texts. One of the most important pieces of archaeological evidence on the topic is a slab of marble from Halicarnassus (Bodrum, Turkey). Currently located at the British Museum, it depicts two female warriors nicknamed "Achillia" and "Amazon". The relief is dated from the period of the 1st or 2nd century AD.. (cited from: https://www.forbes.com/sites/drsarahbond/2017/04/12/female-gladiators-were-a-part-of-the-lure-of-the-roman-arena-too/#20a96812032d and https://www.ancient-origins.net/history-ancient-traditions/gladiatrix-female-fighters-offered-lewd-entertainment-ancient-rome-005272)

The Modern Day Warrior Woman

Do the women in these stories inspire you? A modern day Warrior Woman does not necessarily have to fight alongside men in battle and war.

Women have been considered the lesser sex, or thought of as weak for thousands of years. Now however, women are successfully working in non-traditional fields such as engineering, forensic science, construction and as CEOs of large corporations. There are female experts in every imaginable field and their offices are often full of pictures of their horses!

A warrior woman possess a determined spirit, a "can do" attitude, that drives her actions towards her goals. She is not afraid to explain her position again and again until her audience understands that she won't go silent. She sees no task too hard. She is powerful inside and out. She has the confidence that she can move mountains and, in the face of difficulty, her resolve becomes stronger.

A woman who rides horses knows that she cannot control the strength of a horse but, by getting to know the horse, and learning to ask the horse to respond to cues, she creates a partnership with the horse. Learning to channel the power of a horse is very empowering!

Female equestrians of today are much like the Warrior Women of the past; they are drawn to horses because of their desire to learn how to develop cooperative leadership of things that are more powerful than they perceive themselves.

The Warrior Women of today are in board rooms and raising families. They have an inner strength and, in the case of women who ride horses, they have the ability to work with a powerful animal that totally relies on their cues. If you don't believe that, try telling a woman she is incapable as she gallops towards you on a thousand pound horse!

Are you horse lover that fits the profile of he Warrior Woman ? ....be strong!

Check all boxes that apply. Then write out how you exhibit those qualities in your life.

- ☐ Do you have a "can do" attitude?
- ☐ Do you work in a non-traditional field?
- ☐ Are you an expert in your field?
- ☐ Are you goal-oriented?
- ☐ Do you speak out when others are afraid to or when you are not understood?
- ☐ Are you confident?
- ☐ Do you create partnerships?
- ☐ Are you a leader?
- ☐ Do you have inner strength?

You're a Warrior Woman!

_____
_____
_____
_____
_____

Queens

Queen Elizabeth has been a rider almost since she could walk. Many members of her royal family are horse enthusiasts. Her great-grandfather, King Edward VII, and father, King George, were both racehorse owners. The Queen Mother was enamored with National Hunt racing. The queen's daughter, Princess Anne, and granddaughter, Zara Phillips, were both world-class eventers and Princes William and Harry are both accomplished polo players. (cited from: https://www.cheatsheet.com/entertainment/revealed-queen-elizabeths-amazing-history-with-royal-racehorses.html/)

The Royals around the world have been horse breeders and horse lovers for centuries Much of the creation and preservation of horse breeds was established by Kings and Queens of ages past.

Queen Laxmibai

By the time Laxmibai was a teenager, she had already violated many of the expectations for women in India's patriarchal society. She could read and write. She had learned to ride a horse and wield a sword. But where those spirited ways might have been scorned in another young Indian woman, they would prove to serve her well as she went on to leave an indelible mark on Indian history.

In the mid-19th century, what became the modern nation of India was dotted with hundreds of princely states, one of which, Jhansi, in the north, was ruled by Queen Laxmibai. Her reign came at a pivotal time: The British, who were expanding their presence in India, had annexed her realm and stripped her of power. Laxmibai tried to regain control of Jhansi through negotiations, but when her efforts failed she joined the Indian Rebellion of 1857, an uprising of soldiers, landowners, townspeople and others against the British in what is now known as India's first battle for independence. It would be 90 years before the country would finally uproot the British, in 1947.

The queen, or rani, went on to train and lead her own army, composed of both men and women. In the decades that followed, her life became a subject of competing narratives. Indians hailed her as a heroine, the British as a wicked, Jezebel-like figure. But somewhere between these portrayals she emerged as a symbol not just of resistance but of the complexities associated with being a powerful woman in India. Laxmibai wasn't of royal blood. Manakarnika, as she was named at birth, is widely believed to have been born in 1827 in Varanasi, a city in northeast India on the banks of the Ganges River. She was raised among the Brahmin priests and scholars who sat atop India's caste system. Her father worked in royal courts as an adviser, giving her access to an education, as well as horses. In 1842, Manakarnika married Maharaja Gangadar Rao, the ruler of Jhansi, and took on the name Laxmibai

By most accounts she was an unconventional queen, and a compassionate one. She refused to abide by the norms of the purdah system, under which women were concealed from public view by veils or curtains. She insisted on speaking with her advisers and British officials face to face. She wore a turban, an accessory more common among men. She is said to have trained women in her circle to ride and fight. She attended to the poor, regardless of their caste, a practice that even today would be considered bold in parts of India. While she was queen, the powerful British East India Company was beginning to seize more land and resources. In 1848, Lord Dalhousie, India's governor general, declared that princely states with leaders lacking natural born heirs would be annexed by the British under a policy called the Doctrine of Lapse. Laxmibai's only child had died, and her husband's health was starting to deteriorate. The couple decided to adopt a 5-year-old boy to groom as successor to the throne, and hoped that the British would recognize his authority despite the declaration. Soon after her husband died, in 1853, the East India Company offered the queen a pension if she agreed to cede control. She refused, exclaiming: "Meri Jhansi nahin dungee" ("I will not give up my Jhansi") — a Hindi phrase that to this day is etched into India's memory, stirring up feelings of pride and patriotism.

Beyond Jhansi's borders, a rebellion was brewing as the British imposed their social and Christian practices and banned Indian customs. The uprising spread from town to town, reaching Jhansi in June 1857. Dozens of British were killed in the ensuing massacre by the rebels. The British turned on Laxmibai, accusing her of conspiring with the rebels to seek revenge over their refusal to recognize her heir. Whether or not she did remains disputed. Some accounts insist that she was wary of the rebels and that she had even offered to protect British women and children during the violence.

Tensions escalated, and in early 1858 the British stormed Jhansi's fortress. "Street fighting was going on in every quarter," Dr. Thomas Lowe, the army's field surgeon, wrote in his 1860 book Central India During the Rebellion of 1857 and 1858. " Heaps of dead lay all along the rampart and in the streets below. Those who could not escape," he added, "threw their women and babies down wells and then jumped down themselves."

As the town burned, the queen escaped on horseback with her son, Damodar, tied to her back. In the end, the British took the town, leaving 3,000 to 5,000 people dead, and hoisted the British flag atop the palace. Left with no other options, Laxmibai decided to join the rebel forces and began training an army in the nearby state of Gwalior.

The British troops, close on her heels, attacked Gwalior on a scorching summer morning in June 1858. She led a counter charge clad in the attire of a man, mounted on horseback, and was killed. It was the last battle in the Indian Rebellion. "The Indian Mutiny had produced but one man," Sir Hugh Rose, the leader of the British troops, reportedly said when fighting ended, "and that man was a woman." The violence left thousands dead on both sides. The British government dissolved the East India Company over concerns about its aggressive rule and brought India under the control of the crown. It then reversed Lord Dalhousie's policy of annexing kingdoms without heirs.

Today, Queen Laxmibai of Jhansi has been immortalized in India's nationalist narrative. There are movies, TV shows, books and even nursery rhymes about her. Streets, colleges and universities are named after her. Young girls dress up in her likeness, wearing pants, turbans and swords. Statues of her on horseback, with her son tied to her back, have been erected in many cities throughout India. Almost a century after her death, the Indian National Army formed an all-female unit that aided the country in its battle for independence in the 1940s. It was called the Rani of Jhansi regiment. (cited from: The NY Times, by: By Alisha Haridasani Gupta, 8-14-19)

Queen Isabella of Spain

Queen Isabella had a passion for golden horses. Records show that she kept one hundred pale palomino horses in her stable and reserved the right to own and ride horses of this coloring for nobility. She was so enchanted by these horses that Queen Isabella sent one of her beloved palomino stallions and five mares to her Viceroy in New Spain, now known as Mexico, to breed and spread across the new lands discovered. During 1599 – 1660 Spain's greatest baroque painter, Diego de Silva Velazquez used the Isabella horses many times in his romantically extravagant paintings. These included paintings of King Phillip VI and Queen Isabella of Spain mounted on the beautiful golden horses The paintings of large war scenes captured the dreamy golden Spanish horse with huge, flowing manes, beautifully crested necks and strong round haunches. Isabella horses were presented to the Spanish Lord Juan de Palomino, who marveled at the beauty of the horses. It is thought that this might be where they later received their name of Palomino which has remained in use over the centuries. (cited from: https://baroquehorse.com.au/history-of-the-isabella-horse/)

It was this famous queen that financed the voyages of Christopher Columbus. On his second voyage, in 1493, there were thirteen hundred adventurers made up of cavalry and infantry, farm laborers, a wide range of craftsmen, and five ecclesiastics to perform conversions. Queen Isabella mandated that Columbus bring horses to the new land for the first time along with cattle, other livestock, grains and seeds but there were no women. (cited from: https://www.americanheritage.com/everything-you-need-know-about-columbus)

Marie Henrietta of Austria, Queen of the Belgians

Marie Henrietta of Austria was born on August 23, 1836 as the daughter of Archduke Joseph, Palatine of Hungary, and Duchess Maria Dorothea of Württemberg. She was described as, "having been raised as a boy." Marie Henrietta learned to speak German, French, English and Italian. She was musically gifted and played the piano and the harp. She rode horses like a professional!

Empress Elisabeth of Austria

"Sisi", as she was known, was born on December 24, 1837. She was a fervent horsewoman, she rode every day for hours on end, becoming probably the world's best, as well as best-known, female equestrian. Newspapers published articles on her passion for riding sports, diet and exercise regimens. She was obsessively concerned with maintaining her youthful figure and beauty, which were already legendary during

her life. While traveling in Geneva in 1898, she was mortally wounded by an Italian anarchist named Luigi Luchen. (cited from: http://ridingaside.blogspot.com/2011/11/empress-elisabeth-of-austria.html)

Catherine the Great

Catherine II was the Empress of Russia from 1762-1796. She is one of the most powerful women in European history. In 1745, she converted to Russian Orthodoxy and married Grand Duke Peter of Russia. As Empress, she became known as Catherine the Great and, in the role, she expanded and modernized the Russian Empire.

Equestrian portrait of Catherine the Great in uniform of the Preobrazhensky Regiment one of the oldest Imperial Russian guard units circa 1762.

There is a well-known legend surrounding Empress Catherine the Great of Russia, and it involves a horse. The myth is that Catherine was crushed to death by a horse while attempting to have sex with it. The truth is that Catherine did not die while attempting sex  with a horse. The truth appears to be that Catherine died in bed of illness. So how did the myth arise? During past centuries the easiest way for people to offend and verbally attack their female enemies was sex. Historians believe the horse myth originated in France, among the French upper classes, soon after Catherine's death, as a way to mar her legend since France and Russia were great rivals.

Catherine spent much of her early married life riding her horse. She refused to ride side-saddle and wrote, "The more violent the exercise, the more I enjoyed it." (cited from: https://www.vortexmag.net/en/the-strange-story-about-catherine-the-great-and-her-horse/)

Empress Augusta-Viktoria

The first wife of Wilhelm II, German Emperor and King of Prussia, Augusta Victoria of Schleswig-Holstein-Sonderburg-Augustenburg was born on October 22, 1858, in Dolzig Palace in Sommerfeld, Prussia (now Lubsko, Poland). She was the great-niece of Queen Victoria. Augusta Victoria was the last German Empress and Queen of Prussia.

Her husband enjoyed exercise out of doors. The queen shared all of his pastimes with him because she believed in fresh air and had a horror of getting stout. When they were first married she rarely let a day go by without riding or driving with the emperor. In Berlin they were often seen riding their horses or driving in the park. She had her own stables, selected her horses, and gave her own orders governing them. When younger she said that she never saw a horse she was afraid to mount and the harder they were to govern the better she liked them. She is one of the few queens who was a member of a royal guard, and she could go through a drill as well as a man. (cited from: https://mrsdaffodildigresses.wordpress.com/tag/queen-marie-henriette-of-belgium/)

Princess Cecilie of Mecklenburg-Schwerin Crown Princess of Germany and Prussia

On June 6, 1905, Cecilie married Crown Prince Wilhelm. She was the last German Crown Princess and Crown Princess of Prussia. Princess Cecilie had many tastes in common with her husband right from the start. They were both excellent equestrians and she could hold her own with him in managing the wildest horses. Her devotion to horses led her to accept the office of patroness of the Society for the Prevention of Cruelty to Animals. She likewise influenced her father-in-law to abolish the bearing rein in the imperial stables. (cited from: https://mrsdaffodildigresses.wordpress.com/tag/queen-marie-henriette-of-belgium/)

Queen Wilhelmina of the Netherlands

Wilhelmina (Wilhelmina Helena Pauline Maria; (August 31, 1880 – November 28, 1962) was Queen regent of the Kingdom of the Netherlands from 1890 to 1948. She was skilled in managing horses. When the queen was a young girl she always begged for the most reckless horses. When the queen mother opposed this she often explained, "No, I must teach them that I am their mistress." (cited from: https://mrsdaffodildigresses.wordpress.com/tag/queen-marie-henriette-of-belgium/)

Empress Alexandra of Russia

Alexandra Feodorovna was born Princess Victoria Alix Helena Louise Beatrice in Darmstadt, Germany, in 1872. At age twelve, Princess Alix met Grand Duke Nicholas Romanov, heir to the Romanov dynasty in Russia. The two developed a relationship and married in 1894

The czarina of Russia had wonderful saddle and driving horses. It was said that she could "mount and dismount with all the ease and grace natural to a well-trained officer." She would ride horseback until the snow and cold forced her into a sleigh. (cited from: https://allthatsinteresting.com/alexandra-feodorovna)

Queen Victoria

Victoria reigned the second longest of any British monarch in history (1837-1901). The current Queen Elizabeth II has reigned longer. Queen Victoria is associated with Great Britain's great age of industrialization, expansion, economic progress, and empire building. It was an era of prosperity and growth and was named for her – "The Victorian Era". Queen Victoria hated the idea of cars in the Mews and said to the Duke of Portland, her Master of the Horse, "I hope you will never allow any of these horrible machines to be used in my stables."

Queen Victoria was an accomplished rider. This painting by Sir Francis Grant records a review which took place on the morning of June 11, 1845 when the Queen inspected the troops stationed at Windsor, the Regiment of Royal Horse Guards and the 2nd Battalion of Coldstream Guards. According to The Times newspaper the following morning, the Queen had worn a blue habit with a velvet collar and a Field-Marshal's aiguillette (ornamental braided cord). In the painting she also wears the ribbon of the Garter and in the background we can see the Duke of Wellington on his horse. The Queen's horse is Hammon, an Arab who had been bred in the King of Prussia's stud at Trakehnen and was given to the Queen in 1844. The horse, according to the Queen, behaved extremely well. (cited from: https://www.rct.uk/collection/400589/queen-victoria-1819-1901-on-horseback)

In this painting by Grant the young, recently crowned Queen is here seen riding on her horse Comus, with her dogs, Dash and Islay in front, accompanied by her court with a view of the castle in the far distance against a dawn sky. The Queen clearly enjoyed the creation of this very personal painting, just as she enjoyed riding out with these companions, On July 31, 1839 her journal describes Lord Melbourne sitting on a wooden horse within the artist's studio, "looking so funny, his white hat on, an umbrella, in lieu of a stick in one hand, and holding the reins, which were fastened to the steps, in the other." (cited from: https://www.rct.uk/collection/400749/queen-victoria-1819-1901-riding-out)

Her death in 1901 stunned the nation. What followed was chaos and confusion and of course...horses! There was no one alive who could remember how to bury a monarch and the Queen had asked for a full military state funeral. Previous royal funerals had been private candlelit affairs, taking place at night, but this queen had requested a full military state funeral. No embalming, no lying-in-state, no mourning black; she wanted a white funeral, purple and white, with white ponies and a gun carriage and the first burial of a monarch outside the confines of Westminster Abbey and St George's Chapel since George I in 1727. On February 1, 1901, the cortege crossed the Solent, flanked by eleven miles of battleships and cruisers, each booming out their guns as the tiny yacht, Alberta, passed by, bearing the queen's coffin. The cortege remained in the harbor overnight and proceeded by train to London's Victoria station in the early hours of February 2. Then came the final train journey to Windsor, where the procession waited as the coffin was placed on the gun carriage. More complications followed when the horses, having stood motionless in the freezing weather, suddenly kicked and broke away from their traces, almost toppling the coffin to the ground. The front of the procession had already marched off and reached the end of Windsor Street before it could be stopped and turned around. The Royal Horse Artillery were unable to re-harness the horses and disaster loomed. Prince Louis Battenberg (grandfather of Prince Philip, the Duke of Edinburgh) rescued the day, suggesting: "If it is impossible to mend the traces you can always get the naval guard of honor to drag the gun carriage." Accordingly, one hundred thirty eight bluejackets piled their arms (propped up their weapons), attached ropes to the carriage where the harnesses had been, and dragged the gun carriage to St George's Chapel by hand, giving birth to a new royal tradition. (cited from: https://www.historyextra.com/period/victorian/queen-victoria-death-funeral-mask-cause/)

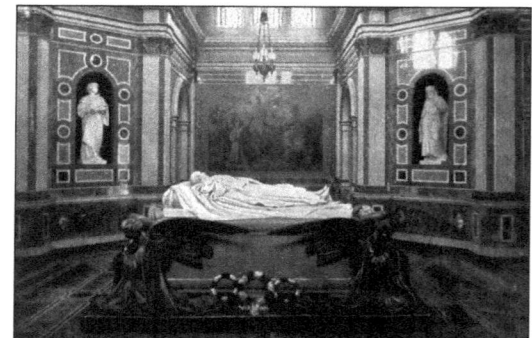

The Mausoleum Where Queen Victoria Was Buried

Queen Elizabeth I

England grew very strong during the reign of Elizabeth (1558 - 1603). It was a time of global discovery. Literature and the arts flourished. Elizabeth was very good at diplomacy and politics and she was able to prevent religious wars and civil war in England.

England lost many horses during the War of the Roses (1455 -1485) so, horses were imported from Italy, Spain and North Africa. Laws in 1541 required that nobles keep certain numbers of horses. Those in the highest positions had to house seven strong trotting horses who were at least three years old and fourteen hands high. The less wealthy had to have at least one acceptable horse. In 1580, the Queen became so concerned about the need for more horses that she established a "Special Commission for the Increase and Breed of Horses". This commission was charged to inspect and rate each stallion and mare throughout England. Elizabeth ordered that a count of horses would be taken every six months "until the realm be replenished with horses."

Elizabeth loved to ride. She would spend many an hour riding fast through the Palace grounds. Her love for the sport terrified her Councilors, who feared that she would seriously injure, or even kill herself, from a fall. But Elizabeth was undaunted and continued to ride long distances and at great speed until the end of her life. Even in her sixties, she could ride a distance of ten miles, even though her Councilors advised the aging Queen to take the carriage. Elizabeth would tire out her ladies by riding hard and, early in her reign, Robert Dudley, her Master of Horse, had to bring over some new horses from Ireland, as the Queen's own horses were not fast or strong enough for her. Elizabeth and Dudley would ride together often. He was probably the most accomplished horse-man in England, and could match the Queen's speed and vigor. (cited from: https://www.elizabethi.org/contents/pastimes/)

Queen Elizabeth II

A lifelong horse lover, the Queen received her first pony at the age of four from her grandfather, King George VI. It was a Shetland pony named Peggy. She was riding the pony by the age of six. By age eighteen, she was an accomplished rider and has continued to ride for pleasure.

The Queen has been spotted on horseback numerous times throughout her reign and sometimes she rides alongside another dignitary. Back in 1982, the Queen rode horses with President Ronald Reagan while he was at Windsor Castle on a state visit.

In her role as monarch, Elizabeth has also ridden in a ceremonial role. From her first appearance as princess in 1947 and throughout her reign as queen until 1986, she attended the annual Trooping the Color ceremony on horseback. Initially, she rode a bay police horse named Tommy in 1947. When her father, King George VI, was unwell, she rode in his place on his chestnut horse Winston (bottom right), and she rode Winston after George VI's death. Later she rode a chestnut horse named Imperial. For eighteen consecutive years, from 1969 to 1986, her horse was a black mare named Burmese. Burmese was a gift from the Royal Canadian Mounted Police. From 1987 onward, since Burmese retired, she has attended in a carriage.

Elizabeth owns many thoroughbred horses for use in racing, having initially inherited the breeding and racing stock of her late father King George VI, in 1952. Up until the late 1960s she raced her own bred stock as well as horses bred by the National Stud. Her registered racing colors (silks), worn by the jockeys riding her race horses, are the same as those used by her father and great-grandfather, King Edward VII; a purple and scarlet jacket with gold braiding, with black cap. As of 2013, horses owned by the Queen have won over sixteen hundred races.

Elizabeth II hosts the Royal Windsor Horse Show every year in Windsor Park, part of the royal estate in Berkshire. She also helps to preserve rare breeds of horses, such as Cleveland Bays. (cited from: https://en.wikipedia.org/wiki/Elizabeth_II%27s_horses)

Queen for a Day

The show, "Queen for a Day", aired on TV and radio from 1947 to 1964. Each episode would consist of three to four women competing to become Queen for a Day. The women revealed their most personal stories to the American public. Audience members then decided which woman's story was most heart-wrenching (by use of the applause-o-meter) and the winner was crowned Queen for a Day. The selected queen was dramatically adorned with a crown, robe and roses. They received gifts such as appliances, fully paid nights out and many, many other prizes,

Most of us will never become queens and the thought of living like one is only a dream. Are you a dreamer who sees yourself riding a horse, with a flowing mane and tail, on beaches or through beautiful, enormous, rolling fields? Do you read books with horses and watch movies with horses? Did you play with toy horses while growing up? Do you dream 24/7 about owning a horse someday? Or do you currently own a horse and you are 100% consumed with love for your horse? All you can think about is your next ride on your beloved horse!

Making dreams come true is not just for TV shows. Many young girls grow up dreaming of owing a horse. They clean stalls in exchange for riding lessons and they save money to buy a horse, even before they buy their first car. What started as a dream, becomes a life long love of all things horse related. And, when that dream finally comes true, you are living the dream! You are not just "Queen for a Day".

Are you a horse lover that fits the profile of Queen for a Day?... follow your dreams!

Check all boxes that apply. Then describe your horse lover dream.

- ☐ Are you a dreamer?
- ☐ Do you envision yourself riding a magnificent horse?
- ☐ Do you read every book about horses that you can get your hands on?
- ☐ Do you watch every horse movie and TV show about horses?
- ☐ If you don't own a horse, do you dream of owning a horse?
- ☐ If you do own a horse, are you consumed with thinking about your wonderful horse all day?
- ☐ Do you try to make your dreams come true?

You're living the dream as "Queen for a Day"!

_____
_____
_____
_____
_____
_____
_____

Deities and Mythology

A deity is a god or goddess that is revered as supremely powerful or benevolent. Gods and goddesses are found in Greek and Roman mythology as well as the mythology of many other cultures

The gods of the ancient Greek pantheon are divided into various categories. The first of these--the Olympian gods, Titan gods and primordial gods--represent the three generations of deities to rule the cosmos. The next five categories divide the gods by domain, namely the gods of sky, sea, earth and underworld. The final category is the daemones--minor deities or spirits representing abstract ideas, emotions and conditions--and apotheosised mortals.
(cited from: https://www.theoi.com/greek-mythology/greek-gods.html)

Greek and Roman mythology often have the same gods but with different names because many Roman gods are borrowed from Greek mythology but often with different traits. The Hippoi Athanatoi were the immortal horses of the gods. Most of these divine steeds were offspring of the four Anemoi (Wind-Gods) who themselves drew the chariot of Zeus in the guise of horses.

There were thousands of gods and goddesses worshiped throughout ancient China as well. Each town, village, city, field, farm, and sometimes even separate plot in a graveyard, had its own Tudi Gong, an elemental earth spirit, who was recognized and honored. There were also spirits known as Kuei-Shen, nature spirits, who might inhabit a tree or live by a stream or preside over a garden. (cited from: https://www.ancient.eu/article/894/most-popular-gods--goddesses-of-ancient-china/)

The Celts also had gods and goddesses. Celtic deities can belong to two categories: general deities and local deities. "General deities" were known by Celts throughout large regions and are the gods and goddesses invoked for protection, healing, luck and honor. The "local deities", that embodied Celtic nature worship, were the spirits of a particular feature of the landscape, such as mountains, trees or rivers and thus were generally only known by the locals in the surrounding areas.(cited from: https://en.wikipedia.org/wiki/List_of_Celtic_deities)

Many other cultures had gods and goddesses as well. In Norse mythology, the giants came first and then the Old Gods (the Vanir) and later the New Gods (the Aesir). Ancient Egyptian gods are recorded on tombs and manuscripts beginning in about 2600 BC and lasting until the Romans conquered Egypt in 33 BC. The Late Postclassic period Aztec culture of Mesoamerica (1110–1521 AD) worshiped more than two hundred different deities spanning three broad classes of Aztec life—the heavens,

fertility, agriculture and war. The Maya predate the Aztec and, like the Aztec, based some of their theology on the existing pan-Mesoamerican religions. Among the most ancient of cultures, the people of Babylon developed a diverse melting pot of deities, derived from the older Mesopotamian cultures. Literally, thousands of gods are named in Sumerian and Akkadian, some of the oldest writing on the planet. (cited from: https://www.learnreligions.com/list-of-gods-and-goddesses-by-culture-118503)

Since horses were considered to be strong and powerful, they were often depicted as the faithful and necessary partner of the god or goddess.

Eos (Greek) Aurora (Roman)

Eos was the Greek goddess of the dawn. She was depicted driving a chariot drawn by winged horses. At the close of night she rose from the couch of her beloved Tithonus and, on a chariot drawn by the swift horses, Lampus and Phaëton, she ascended up to heaven from the river Oceanus to announce the coming light of the sun to the gods as well as to mortals. Eos not only announces the coming Helios (god of the sun), but accompanies him throughout the day. Her career is not complete till the evening. (cited from: https://www.theoi.com/Titan/Eos.html)

Eos

Aurora is the Roman name for the goddess of the dawn. Her mythology and attributes are the same as the Greek Eos and she does not seem to have any specifically Roman mythology. Her name simply means the dawn, daybreak or sunrise. (cited from: http://www.thaliatook.com/OGOD/aurora.php)

Aurora

Hera

Hera is the wife of Zeus and the Greek goddess of women, marriage, family and childbirth. She was the Queen of the Gods. Despite her husband's affairs, she stayed with him and ruled by his side. She often misused her position and powers to punish Zeus's lovers but also used her benevolent authority to protect others. One such person was Achilles.

Achilles' stallions were named Balius and Xanthus. The horses, who were immortal, were given by Poseidon as a wedding gift to Achilles' father Peleus. Peleus then gave the horses to Achilles to draw his chariot when his son left home for the Trojan War. The horses' immortal nature made them difficult to control. Automedon, Achilles' charioteer, states that only Patroclus (a close friend of Achilles) was able to fully control these horses. Patroclus used to feed and groom the horses. Patroclus was killed in battle and Xanthus and Balius stood motionless on the field of battle and wept. When Xanthus was rebuked by the grieving Achilles for allowing Patroclus to be slain, Hera granted Xanthus human speech, which broke divine law, allowing the horse to say that a god had killed Patroclus and warn Achilles that a god would soon kill him too.

Diana

Diana was the goddess of the hunt, the moon and nature. She is associated with wild animals and woodland and has the power to talk to and control animals. As goddess of the moon, the ancients believed that every evening she mounted her moon chariot and drove her pure white horses across the heavens She was worshiped at a festival on August 13 called Nemoralia, the Festival of Torches during which worshipers of Diana would form a procession of torches and candles around the dark waters of the sacred Lacus Nemorensis, a forest-buried lake. The lights of their candles and torches joined the light of the moon reflecting upon the surface of the water. During the Festival of Nemoralia it was forbidden to hunt and kill animals. (cited from: http://www.talesbeyondbelief.com/roman-gods/diana.htm)

Rhiannon

In Welsh mythology, Rhiannon is a horse goddess. Rhiannon was married to Pwyll, the Lord of Dyfed. When Pwyll first saw her, she appeared as a golden goddess upon a magnificent white horse. Rhiannon managed to outrun Pwyll for three days. She allowed him to catch up, at which point she told him she would be happy to marry him because it would keep her from marrying Gwawl, who had tricked her into an engagement.

Primarily though, Rhiannon is associated with the horse which appears prominently in much of Welsh and Irish mythology. Many parts of the Celtic world, Gaul in particular, used horses in warfare and so it is no surprise that these animals turn up in the myths and legends of Ireland and Wales. (cited from: https://www.learnreligions.com/rhiannon-horse-goddess-of-wales-2561707)

Epona

Epona was also a Celtic goddess. Her name comes from the Celtic, "epos" meaning "horse" and the suffix "-ona" simply means "on". Epona is the patron goddess of mares and foals. She occupied an important place in the Gallic religion because the horse itself was important in the life of the Gauls. The veneration of the goddess logically then persisted in the army. Yet everything suggests that the common people adored her in rural areas. (cited from: https://www.ancient.eu/article/153/epona/) She was the only Gallo-Celtic goddess that made her way into literature of the Roman Empire. She was highly worshiped by Roman cavalrymen. Almost every Roman stable had a shrine to her. As a deified horsewoman, she is usually portrayed as riding a white mare side-saddle, sometimes with a foal, or sometimes pictured standing while surrounded by horses. (cited from: https://www.ancient.eu/article/153/epona/)

Arion

In order to escape from the pursuit of Poseidon, the goddess, Demeter had metamorphosed herself into a mare. Poseidon deceived her by assuming the figure of a horse and Demeter afterwards gave birth to the horse Arion. He was an extremely swift horse who was endowed with the gift of speech.

Aife (Aiofe)

Aife is a goddess in Irish and Scottish mythology. She is the queen of the Isle of Shadow. She ran a school for warriors although she is not as well known as her sister Scathach. Aife was not vulnerable to magic and commanded a legion of fierce horsewomen. She stole an alphabet of knowledge from the deities to give to humankind. For that infraction, she was transformed into a crane by the elder deities. (cited from: http://godfinder.org/index.html?q=horse)

Astarte

Astarte's name was first recorded about 1478 BC. But her cult was firmly established by then. The cult spread westward from Phoenicia into Greece, Rome and as far as the British Isles. She was the "mistress of horses and chariots". (cited from: https://www.themystica.com/astarte/)

Xatel Ekwa

As a Hungarian sun goddess, like many other ancient solar goddesses, she is linked with horses as she rode through the air on her three steeds. (cited from: https://www.goddess-guide.com/sun-goddesses.html) In Hungarian myth, the world is divided into three spheres: the first is the Upper World (Felső világ), the home of the gods; the second is the Middle World (Középső világ) or world we know, and finally the underworld (Alsó világ). In the center of the world stands a tall tree: the World Tree / Tree of Life (Világfa/Életfa). (cited from: https://en.wikipedia.org/wiki/Hungarian_mythology)

Gna

The Norse goddess Gna has a horse by the name of Hofvarpner that can run through air and water. The sire of this horse is Hamskerper, and its mother is Gardrofa. Gna is the messenger that Frigg sends into the various worlds on her errands.

Étaín Echraide

Étaín Echraide is a heroine of Irish mythology, Her name, Etain Echraide, means "Etain the Horserider". She spent her life being sought by various suitors. In the process she was transformed, at various points, into a worm, a butterfly, a swan and a pool of water. (cited from: https://www.rejectedprincesses.com/princesses/etain

Sanjna

Sanjna is the Hindu goddess of warriors. She disguised herself as a horse and fled from her husband. When he caught her, together they produced the Ashwini Kumaras, the horse twins. Each day the twins bring the dawn as their chariot speeds through the sky.
(cited from: http://godfinder.org/index.html?q=horse)

Mari

Mari is the most important deity in the Basque Mythology. She leads and guides the rest of the deities. She is the queen of Nature and of all its elements. She symbolized Nature and, through her mighty power, she keeps the balance of the natural forces and often times she was seen crossing the sky in a cart pulled by four horses. (cited from: http://basquemythology.amaroa.com/personajes-mitologicos-de-vasconia/mari)

Sol

In the beginning of time, when the cosmos were being created, so too was the Nordic goddess Sol and her brother Mani. Initially, the role of the siblings wasn't clear but, after they created daytime and night, Sol and her brother were assigned their destiny. At a meeting of the existing gods, Sol was anointed the goddess of the sun and Mani god of the moon. Sol was to ride in the sky in a chariot drawn by her horses. (cited from: https://mythology.net/norse/norse-gods/sol/)

Aine

Celtic legends say that Aine was the daughter of Eogabail, who was a member of the legendary Tuatha Dé Danann, a race in Celtic mythology inhabiting Ireland before the arrival of the ancestors of the modern Irish. (cited from: https://www.ancient-origins.net/myths-legends/aine-radiant-celtic-goddess-love-summer-and-sovereignty-007097)

The Tuatha Dé Danann in John Duncan's "Riders of the Sidhe."

Niamh

Niamh is the Celtic goddess of beauty and brightness. She is the daughter of Fand and of Manannán mac Lir, one of the Queens of Tir na nóg. On her magical horse, Embarr, she crossed the Western Sea to ask Fionn mac Cumhail if his son Oisín would come with her to Tír na nóg. Tír na nÓg was an island located beyond the western edge of the known world. The name translates as "Land of Eternal Youth" and is one of the otherworld places where the goddesses and gods of the Tuatha de Danann went when their time as deities had passed. Happiness was the only reality on this island where all enjoyed eternal youth, pleasure, wisdom and peace. Music and beauty were highly valued and always available in the "Land of Eternal Youth". Yet Tír na nÓg was not a place where souls went after death. It could only be reached, while living, by undertaking a difficult journey or by invitation. The tale of Niamh and her love for Oisin, the great warrior poet of ancient Ireland, is the most well known tale of Tír na nÓg. (cited from: https://feminismandreligion.com/2016/04/27/niamh-of-the-golden-hair-by-judith-shaw/)

Penthesilea Queen of the Amazons

The Amazons were a legendary race of warrior women. Penthesilea's reign as their queen was during the years of the Trojan War. The Amazons did not take a particular side in the war and Penthesiliea made an effort to stay away from the conflict. However, when Achilles killed the Trojan prince, Hector, Penthesilea decided that it was time for the Amazons to intervene, so she led the Amazons into war.

It is written that she blazed through the Greeks like lightning. She wanted to prove that the Amazons were great warriors. She wanted to kill Achilles to avenge the death of Hector, and she wanted to die in battle. Although Penthesilea was a ferocious warrior, her life came to an end, at the hands of Achilles. While he was drawn to her with the intention of killing her, he fell in love with her upon seeing her eyes and as his sword struck, Achilles was overcome with enormous grief and regret. (cited from: https://www.ancient-origins.net/myths-legends/dramatic-life-and-death-penthesilea-queen-amazons-002104)

The Kingdom of the Amazons, Book of Treasures (ca.1230-1294) Preserved in the National Library of Russia, Saint Petersburg

The Valkyries

The Valkyries of Norse mythology were women of vast prestige and power. They were one of the few factions of warrior women from ancient lore recognized as having any power over the mortal realm. Known as beacons of strength, they descended from the sky garbed in the feathers of swans coated with sturdy, iron chain-mail, their faces protected by helmets and their spears held aloft fearlessly. Upon the backs of their ethereal horses they came from the heavens to the mortal realm. When seen by the male soldiers on the ground, both awe and terror would sweep the battlefield since their role was to determine the fate of fallen warriors.

Despite this overwhelming awe, it is the duty of the Valkyries not to participate

Found at Tissø, shows a Valkyrie to the left and shieldmaiden to the right.

Stone from Tjängvide, Alskog, Gotland.

in the wars of mortals or to have a role in the physical or mental acts of battle, but rather to choose from the fallen humans who was worthy enough to ascend to the halls of Odin and who was benign enough to be sent to the fields of Freya. Odin's hall, Valhalla, holds the spirits of the warriors in constant training. Their sole purpose in the afterlife is to prepare for the battle that will be the end of the world, Ragnarök, and to defend their universe as best they can from Loki and his army. The fields of Freya, on the other hand, are just as worthy a place to be taken, however the life of the dead there is simple and easy. (cited from: https://www.ancient-origins.net/myths-legends-europe/powerful-valkyries-icons-female-force-and-fear-003407)

Modern Day Goddess

In mythological stories of goddesses, the horse was seen to be strong and powerful. Horses were often depicted as the faithful and necessary partner of the god or goddess. Today, there are some horse owners who see their partnership with powerful horses as a sign of self-importance and status. People like this in the horse world are often called "Divas". This type of horse owner is not looked upon in awe like the goddesses in mythology. Unlike Warrior Women, who see the horse as their partner and have a desire to learn cooperative leadership, divas look to horses to make themselves appear to be important and powerful.

Is there something about owning a horse that makes someone feel like a diva? People who feel like this often rely on outside factors to define themselves. A horse is very strong and powerful and thus, could make a person feel powerful and important too. Let's meet some "Divas" of the horse world.

If you can't Enchant them with Excellence....

☐ **The Know-It-All**
This person knows more than the vet, the trainer and the horse show judge. They have an opinion on everything and will be sure to let everyone else know what they are doing wrong and of course, how to do it correctly.

☐ **The Poor Sport**
If this person is not getting the blue ribbon they are not happy. Either the judge is wrong or it's the trainer's fault or the horse's fault; it is never their fault! They are constantly buying new horses or barn jumping from trainer to trainer to achieve the (impossible) goal of all blue ribbons all the time.

Blind them with Bling!

☐ **The "Arm Chair Quarterback"**
This person never actually participates in anything horse related whether it be cleaning stalls or actually riding. But of course they know about all of it and can tell everyone else how to do it. In reality, they are often afraid of horses.

☐ **The Breed and Discipline Snob**
In a barn full of backyard horses that go trail riding, the owner of the lone horse with registration papers attends horse shows and looks down their nose at all of the other horses owners.

☐ **The Fashionista**
This person never gets dirty - because they actually never do an of the "nitty gritty" work with their horse. Their horse is standing in the aisle, ready for them to ride when they arrive.

Are you a horse lover that fits the profile of a Goddess.?......*don't be a goddess!*

Trendsetters and Reformers

Historically, women's equestrian fashion has mirrored the role of women in society at the time. Before the 14th century, women often rode astride, but from the 1380s onwards riding sidesaddle began to be associated with female virtue and purity, particularly if she was of noble birth. These ideas persisted into the late 19th and early 20th centuries. Women wishing to ride astride were described as "mad, ignorant ungraceful desperadoes" and "violating the laws of good taste."

Bicycle riding for women became popular in the 1890s, prompting changes in women's fashion. Horse riding fashions were much slower to change however, particularly in the very conservative United Kingdom and American east coast where horse riding was often associated with the upper classes. American women were granted the right to vote in 1920 and with these rights began a gradual shift in the general views surrounding women's liberty. The American West led the charge towards this new world, with the LA Times declaring that "the sidesaddle is a cruel burden on a horse and all right-thinking people believe its time is past."(cited from: https://www.stylemyride.net/single-post/2015/08/31/History-of-Equestrian-Fashion-1920s-to-1940s)

Trendsetters are people who can spot new trends early on and spread these fads to new locations and social groups. Sometimes they even create their own trends that others adopt. "Trends" can be almost anything however, fashion trends are the most common type people follow. Many equestrians of the past were trendsetters causing equine fashion to be emulated in every day life. Many trendsetters end up effecting reform too! They often feel that some changes are essential in society. They bring changes in society by persuading people to give up old practices and adopt a new way of life.

Lady Godiva

Lady Godiva was an 11th century noblewoman married to Leofric, the powerful Earl of Mercia and Lord of Coventry. As the story goes, Godiva was troubled by the crippling taxes Leofric had levied on the citizens of Coventry. After she repeatedly asked him to lessen the burden, Leofric quipped that he would lower taxes only if she rode naked on horseback through the center of town. Determined to help the public, Godiva stripped off her clothes, climbed on her horse and galloped through the market square with only her long flowing hair to cover herself. Before leaving, she ordered the people of Coventry to remain inside their homes and not peek, but one man, named Tom, couldn't resist opening his window to get an eyeful. Upon doing so, this "Peeping Tom" was struck blind. After finishing her naked ride, Godiva confronted her husband and demanded that he hold up his end of the bargain. True to his word, Leofric reduced the people's debts.

Coventry, UK

While most historians consider her nude horseback ride a myth, Lady Godiva, or "Godgifu" as some sources call her, was indeed a real person from the 11th century. The historical Godiva was known for her generosity to the church, and along with Leofric, she helped found a Benedictine monastery in Coventry. Contemporary accounts of her life note that Godgifu was one of only a few female landowners in England in the 1000s, but they make no mention of a clothes-free horseback ride. That story appears to have first cropped up some one hundred years after her death in a book by the English monk Roger of Wendover, who was known for stretching the truth in his writings. The legend of "Peeping Tom," meanwhile, didn't become a part of the tale until the 16th century. The Godiva myth was later popularized in songs and in verse by the likes of Alfred, Lord Tennyson, who wrote a famous poem called "Godiva" in 1840. (cited from: https://www.history.com/news/who-was-lady-godiva)

The Long Riders

With the rise of feudalism and patriarchal politics in the Middle Ages, the need to secure a male heir was an affair of state and protecting the virginity of a potential royal bride became increasingly vital. One way to protect the accidental loss of virginity, was to prohibit aristocratic girls from riding astride. Thus sidesaddle riding was introduced into England in 1382 when Princess Anne of Bohemia traveled across Europe via this new mode of equine transport in order to wed King Richard II. For the next two centuries the sidesaddle became increasingly associated with "proper" behavior, until by 1600 riding astride was no longer something a "lady" would do. An unwritten law stated that only a woman as masculine as an Amazon or as heretical as Joan of Arc, would have dared to ride astride.

But as knowledge of the world grew, people wanted to explore the world. Long Riders were among these explorers. Long Riders are men and women who ride more than one thousand continuous miles on a single equestrian journey. English Long Rider Isabella Bird ventured to Hawaii in the late 19th century. There she learned to ride astride thanks to her Hawaiian hosts. In addition to rounding up the wild cattle imported by the King of that island, the Mexican vaqueros had also taught the local women to ride astride. Bird not only adopted this technique, she then used her vaquero saddle when she later explored the Rocky Mountains, Japan, Persia and Tibet on horseback.

Similarly, when Ethel Tweedie left London, she had not planned to forsake the sidesaddle. Yet like Isabella, upon her arrival in Iceland, Ethel discovered that the local women rode astride like their male relations. "Necessity gives courage in emergencies, so I determined to throw aside conventionality, and do in 'Iceland as the Icelanders do.' The amusement of our party when I overtook them, and boldly trotted past, was intense; but I felt so comfortable in my altered seat that their derisive and chaffing remarks failed to disturb me. Riding man-fashion is less tiring than on a side-saddle, and I soon found it far more agreeable, especially when traversing rough ground. My success soon inspired Miss T. to summon up courage and follow my lead. Society is a hard task-master, yet for comfort and safety, I say ride like a man," Tweedie recalled in her book, "A Girl's Ride in Iceland" (1889). (cited from: https://www.horsetalk.co.nz/2014/10/06/sidesaddles-suffragettes-fight-ride-vote/)

Katherine Hepburn

Katharine Hepburn routinely wore slacks on film and cultivated a somewhat genderless image. She was considered far ahead of her time both in terms of fashion and in her outspoken determination to dress for herself instead of dressing only to impress men. Hepburn famously protested a studio decision to replace her usual slacks with a skirts by walking around the studio in her underwear until her slacks were returned. (cited from: https://www.stylemyride.net/single-post/2015/08/31/History-of-Equestrian-Fashion-1920s-to-1940s)

Elizabeth Taylor

National Velvet is the story of a twelve-year-old, horse-crazy girl, Velvet Brown (Elizabeth Taylor), who lives in the small town of Sewels in Sussex, England. In the 1944 movie, Velvet wins a spirited gelding, that she names Pie, in a raffle and decides to train him for the Grand National steeplechase. In the story Velvet decides to wear jockey silks and intends to race him herself. Velvet and Pie clear all hurdles and win the race. Elated but exhausted, Velvet falls off her mount at the finish. After the track doctor discovers that Velvet is a girl, Velvet and Pie are disqualified. Velvet, who expected to be disqualified, only wanted to prove that Pie was a champion. Her functional, "glass ceiling-shattering" wardrobe included a series of chic, high-waist jodhpurs.

Inez Milholland

Born in New York in 1886, Milholland was the eldest daughter of John and Jean Milholland. Her father, a New York Tribune reporter and editorial writer, eventually headed a pneumatic mail tube business that afforded his family a privileged life in both New York and London.

The summer after her sophomore year at Vassar, Inez Milholland became more than an active and energetic student. During a stay in London she became an ardent political radical through her association with the aristocratic suffragette Emmeline Pankhurst. Since discussion of suffrage was forbidden on Vassar's campus, toward the end of her junior year, Milholland helped draw fifty six people out to the small cemetery adjacent to the college for a suffrage meeting. This meeting signaled the beginning of the Vassar Votes for Women Club, which continued to meet off-campus under Milholland's leadership.

After her graduation in 1909, Milholland made her first appearance as a suffrage orator, stopping a New York campaign parade for President William Howard Taft when she began speaking through a megaphone from a window in a building the parade was passing. As she spoke hundreds of men broke ranks to see and hear her, thus beginning her reputation as one of the most powerful, persuasive and beautiful orators in the suffrage movement. In the same year, Milholland applied to the law schools at Yale, Harvard, and Columbia only to be rejected on the basis of her sex. Eventually, she entered the New York University School of Law from which she received a law degree in 1912.

In 1913 the twenty seven-year-old suffragist made her most memorable public appearance. She helped organize a s massive suffrage parade in Washington D.C. scheduled for the day before President Woodrow Wilson was inaugurated. Milholland cemented her charismatic identity as she led the parade, riding atop a large white horse, through crowds of drunken men, wearing a crown and a long white cape. Delivering an address on a tour in Los Angeles on October 19, 1916, Milholland suddenly collapsed. She was hospitalized and ten weeks later the thirty-year-old activist died, her collapse and deterioration a result of pernicious anemia.(cited from: http://vcencyclopedia.vassar.edu/alumni/inez-milholland.html)

Lady Seymour Dorothy Worsley

Seymour Fleming was married at the age of seventeen to Sir Richard Worsley, Seventh Baron of Appuldurcombe House. He mistreated and abused her to a degree that made her elope with her lover, Captain George Bisset six years later.

In the most famous and striking painting of Lady Worsley by Joshua Reynolds (1776), Lady Worsley wears a red riding habit that is clearly inspired by men's uniforms. In general, women were painted in house or garden settings, usually with their husbands or children so that these depictions of power and confidence were still rather exceptional.

Seymour Fleming

Ruins of Appuldurcombe House

Wearing military inspired clothing was a trend among women in the 18th century. This trend was not just a whim of fashion, but it was also an early form of power dressing in breaking through the gender specific dress code. (cited from: https://www.epochs-of-fashion.com/fashion-icons-in-history/seymour-fleming-lady-worsley-and-military-fashion/)

Sir Richard Worsley

Catherine "Skittles" Walters

Catherine Walters (June 13, 1839 – August 4, 1920) was a fashion trendsetter and the last of the great courtesans of Victorian London. She was known as a brilliant horsewoman and drew crowds of sightseers as she rode through Hyde Park. Aristocratic ladies sought to copy whatever habit she wore. She spent an hour a day tightening her corset to make her already small nineteen inch waist slim down to sixteen inches! Wherever she rode suddenly became the most popular place to promenade.

It is not known where she first learned to ride; one of the great passions of her life. One story is that she worked for a time as a bare-back rider in a traveling circus. Perhaps she saw a horse as a child and fell in love with the horses and wanted to ride. The most credible story is that she had access to the local stables and that she taught herself to ride by helping out in the stables and by exercising the horses.

Her horsemanship, for which she was passionately admired, meant that she found acceptance on the hunting field that she was denied in other social situations. Stories about her daring abound, both on and off the field. She once cleared the eighteen foot water fence at the National Hunt Steeplechase, on a bet, after three other riders tried and failed. She won a hundred pounds for her efforts! (cited from: http://scandalouswoman.blogspot.com/2012/03/skittles-last-victorian-courtesan.html)

Alberta Claire, "The Girl from Wyoming"

In October 1911, "The Girl from Wyoming", as she was known, set off on a journey with her sturdy buckskin pony, Bud, and with her shaggy dog, Micky. Her journey took her from Wyoming to Oregon, south to California, across the deserts of Arizona, and on to a triumphant arrival in New York City. Throughout the course of her long journey, Claire publicly stated that she associated her desire to vote with her right to ride astride. Upon her arrival in New York, Alberta was greeted by Teddy Roosevelt, who praised Clare's courage and urged that women be granted the right to vote. (cited from: https://www.horsetalk.co.nz/2014/10/06/sidesaddles-suffragettes-fight-ride-vote/)

Coco Chanel

Women eager to try riding astride soon found the ideal article of clothing: jodhpurs. Originally designed in Northern India, jodhpurs were introduced into the UK by the popular, newly introduced, sport of polo. Polo was played in India during British colonial rule in the 1830s and British army officers introduced both polo and jodhpurs to the UK in the late 1800s. Jodhpurs were designed to have leather patches on the inside of the leg for protection against saddle rubs and, unlike standard English breeches, jodhpurs continued down to the ankle instead of stopping mid-calf. This design provided better leg protection and also made wearing expensive long boots unnecessary. The design was extremely popular with men for riding both horses and motorcycles in the First World War. The flared hips design was useful for riding in warm climates and also for comfort in the saddle, as stretch fabrics had not yet been invented. Jodhpurs became part of the accepted dress code for riding. (cited from: https://www.stylemyride.net/single-post/2015/08/31/History-of-Equestrian-Fashion-1920s-to-1940s)

Polo Servants in Jodhpurs

Conservative circles may have been scandalized by women adopting jodhpurs, but some women were not willing to wait around until riding astride was universally accepted. Coco Chanel helped to trailblazer women's equestrian fashions in the 1920s by designing her own jodhpurs based on the clothing of the male riders around her. "I gave women a sense of freedom," she once said. "I gave them back their bodies, bodies that were drenched in sweat due to fashion's finery: lace, corsets, underclothes, padding."

Her devotion for horse riding and simple elegance caused Chanel to choose comfortable breeches, riding boots and jackets. The traditional male outfit with white shirt, jacket, vest and trousers was adjusted so it would fit her feminine body. Coco Chanel changed ladies' equestrian fashion in 1920, designing her own breeches on the basis of male riders' outfits that she was seeing every day. Her designs were based on the principle of taking a male outfit and creating truly feminine cut thus recreating it properly while maintaining its elegance, but making it as feminine as possible. During World War I women were still wearing skirts. However, at that time, many women started wearing trousers and uniforms in their workplaces. Chanel started designing women's trousers. Soon, trousers became a conscious choice of women, not just the necessity of war. Chanel, as a fierce lover of horse riding, contributed to revolutionizing ladies' equestrian fashion. Today, we still benefit from her somewhat rebellious approach to horse riding. Equestrianism and all its disciplines remain the only Olympic sport, in which women are in competition with men and the attire is generally the same. (cited from: http://wanthaveit.com/coco-chanel-and-revolution-of-equestrian-fashion/)

Coco Chanel, far left

Young Princess Elizabeth in Jodhpurs

Jodhpurs at the film set

Blazing Trails

When horses were used primarily for work and war, horses were a "boy thing".

Up until the 1900s, women rode sidesaddle and were considered too delicate to ride without the assistance of a groom or hired hand. Women's exposure to horses, for the better part of human history, was limited! But as times changed, the role of the horse changed too. No longer was the horse needed for work and war. The horse became a companion. Once that happened, women discovered that they could bond with these large powerful animals in a way that men could not.

Non-verbal communication skills tend to be more strongly developed in women than in men so women are more easily able to become proficient at understanding horses. This is very empowering! Horses have the ability to give women feelings of power, freedom and independence in many ways.

Some women discovered that power, freedom and independence by blazing trails on horseback, some by starting fashion trends that had previously been deemed unacceptable and some learned to have a voice on issues that they felt were important.

Does the feeling of being able to ride a horse make you feel empowered? Does it give you confidence? Do you feel like you have an exceptional ability to communicate? Do all of these feelings translate into your daily life? If you answered yes to any of these you are a Trendsetter, a Reformer - you are a Trailblazer!

Are you a horse lover that fits the profile of a Trailblazer?......you go girl!

Check all boxes that apply. Then write down how you blaze trails in your life.

- ☐ *Do you have non-verbal communication skills?*
- ☐ *Do you say, "I can do that" when someone says, "that's not something you should be doing"?*
- ☐ *Does being with a horse make you feel empowered?*
- ☐ *Does riding a horse give you a feeling of freedom?*
- ☐ *Does the ability to feel comfortable with horses make you feel confident?*

You are a Trailblazer, a Trendsetter!

_____
_____
_____
_____
_____
_____
_____
_____
_____
_____

Performers

Mae West and Mister Ed

'National Velvet' with Elizabeth Taylor

Horse movies are a lot like dog movies: They usually make you cry, and sometimes they get animal facts wrong. But, there are times that you will see some real horsemanship too! Many of the equine stars of the past and present have been ridden and trained by women. And many stars, like Shirley Temple, owned horses even though they were never seen with horses in movies .

Prairie Rose Henderson

You may not recognize her name, but Prairie Rose Henderson became one of the first professional women athletes in the world in 1899. Born as Ann Robbins in the 1870s, this cowgirl grew up working on a ranch. By the time she was in her late twenties she was one of the foremost cowgirl bronc riders in the Westland ranges.

Women were not allowed to compete in rodeo contests but Rose insisted and since no prohibition was found in the rules, she participated in the Cheyenne Frontier Days, winning a prize saddle. She became known as Prairie Rose Henderson and she made a name for herself on the rodeo circuit. She specialized in bareback bronc riding, relay racing, flat racing, roping and trick riding.

She joined the Irwin Brothers Wild West Show and drew attention across the country with her opulent riding clothes of her own design. They included feathers, sequins, chiffon, a broad-brimmed hat, knee-length bloomers, and of course, cowboy boots. Like most professional riders, Prairie Rose suffered several job-related injuries. One example occurred in 1920. While participating in a Kansas rodeo, the bronc she was riding ran off the grounds and into a tree. Rose's head hit the tree and two of her front teeth were knocked out. Ever the show-woman, she stayed on her saddle and continued riding.

In 1929, she returned to Wyoming, married, and retired from rodeo riding. One fateful night several years later, a blizzard caught Prairie Rose out in the elements, and she was lost until six and a half years later when her skeleton was found by a scouting firefighter. Her identifying mark was a championship belt buckle still worn upon her waist. (cited from: https://texashillcountry.com/saddles-grit-ostrich-feathers-life-of-prairie-rose-henderson/)

Two Gun Nan Aspinwall

Born in New York on February 2, 1880, Nan Aspinwall (1880-1964) spent most of her early years in Nebraska, where her parents were storekeepers in Liberty, a small Gage County town.

By 1899 Nan was performing as an oriental dancer, "Princess Omene". Sometime in 1905 or 1906, she began appearing as the "Montana Girl", an expert horsewoman, roper and sharpshooter and by 1906 she was billed (along with husband Frank Gable) as a "Lariat Expert". The couple performed with the combined Buffalo Bill's Wild West and Pawnee Bill's Far East Troupe. On a bet from Buffalo Bill, she rode on horseback from San Francisco to New York and back in 1911, supporting herself with exhibitions of roping and riding in small towns along the way. Later she and Frank had their own vaudeville show. Photographs and souvenirs of Nan Aspinwall's career as an oriental dancer, sharpshooter, and vaudeville actress fill six scrapbooks in the collections of the Nebraska State Historical Society. (cited from: https://nebraskahistory.pastperfectonline.com/byperson?keyword=Aspinwall%2C+Nan+Jeanne+%22Two-Gun%22%2C+1880-1964)

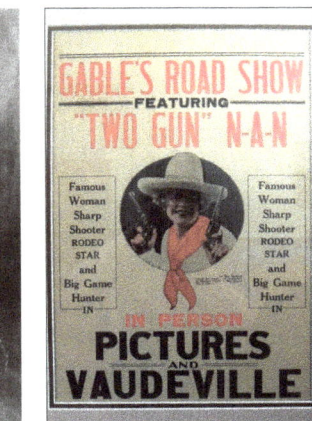

Annie Oakley

Phoebe Ann Moses Butler (1860 – 1926) became known as legendary sharpshooter Annie Oakley.

Annie's father died when she was six. Her mother remarried and shortly after, her new husband passed away too. At the age of eight or nine Annie went to live with Superintendent Edington's family at the Darke County Infirmary in Ohio, which housed the elderly, the orphaned, and the mentally ill. In exchange for helping with the children, Annie received an education and learned the skill of sewing from Mrs. Edington, which she would later use to make her own costumes.

Annie returned home at the age of thirteen. Her mother had remarried a third time but the family still had financial difficulties. Annie used her father's old Kentucky rifle to hunt small game for the Katzenberger brother's grocery store in Greenville, Ohio, where it was resold to hotels and restaurants in Cincinnati, eighty miles away. Annie was so successful at hunting that she was able to pay the $200 mortgage on her mother's house with the money she earned. She was fifteen years old.

Her noted shooting ability brought an invitation from Jack Frost, a hotel owner in Cincinnati who had purchased her game, to participate in a shooting contest against a well-known marksman, Frank E. Butler. Annie won the match with twenty-five shots out of twenty-five attempts. Butler missed one of his shots. This amazing girl entranced Butler, and the two shooters began a courtship that resulted in marriage on August 23, 1876. For the next few years, the Butlers traveled across the country giving shooting exhibitions with their dog, George, as an integral part of the act. It was at this time that Annie adopted the stage name of Oakley.

At a March 1884 performance in St. Paul, Minnesota, Annie befriended the Lakota leader, Sitting Bull and they became good friends. Butler and Oakley joined Buffalo Bill's Wild West in 1885. It was her name, not Frank's, that appeared on the advertising posters as "Champion Markswoman". Butler happily accepted the position as her manager and assistant. Oakley and Butler prospered with the Wild West show and remained with the show for seventeen years. In 1887, Buffalo Bill's Wild West toured England to join in the Golden Jubilee of Queen Victoria and returned to Europe again in 1889. Oakley and Butler's desire for less extensive traveling, as well as a serious train accident that injured her back, caused them to leave the show in 1901. However, she continued to perform and eventually joined another wild west show, "The Young Buffalo Show," in 1911.

The United States was pulled into World War I in 1917 and Oakley offered to raise a regiment of woman volunteers to fight in the war. She had made the same offer during the Spanish-American War; neither time was it accepted. She also volunteered to teach marksmanship to the troops. Oakley gave her time to the National War Council of the Young Men's Christian Association, War Camp Community Service and the Red Cross.

Oakley began making plans for a comeback in 1922. Attracting large crowds in Massachusetts, New York, and major cities, she had planned to star in a motion picture. Unfortunately, at the end of the year, she and Butler were severely injured in an automobile accident. It took Oakley more than a year to recover from her injuries. By 1924, she was performing again, but her recovery did not last long. By 1925, she was frail and in poor health. She and Butler moved to her hometown in Ohio to be near her family. In 1926, after fifty happy years of marriage, the Butlers died. Annie Oakley died on November 3 and Frank Butler died November 21, within three weeks of each other. Both died of natural causes after a long and adventuresome life. (cited from: https://centerofthewest.org/explore/buffalo-bill/research/annie-oakley/)

Annie Oakley, their Dog Dave, and Frank Butler, 1911.

Sonora Webster Carver

Sonora Webster Carver was an American entertainer, widely known for being one of the first female horse divers in the world. She was born on February 2, 1904 to a working-class family in Waycross, Georgia. After seeing an ad placed by circus entertainer William Doc Carver in 1923 that called for "a girl who could swim and dive and was willing to travel," Sonora felt her call, lifting her from a life of "genteel poverty."

Her job as horse diver was to mount a running horse as it reached the top of a forty-foot (sometimes sixty-foot) tower and sail down on its back as it plunged into a tank of twelve-foot-deep water.

Sonora married Doc Carver's son, Al, and shortly after her engagement, she was blinded from retinal displacement during a performance after one of the horses, Red Lips, went into a steep nosedive sending her face-first into the water with her eyes open. She fearlessly continued to dive horses for eleven years until World War II. After leaving the carnival in 1942, she and her husband moved to New Orleans. She learned Braille and worked as a Dictaphone typist until her retirement in 1979. Sonora died at the age of ninety nine after seventy two years of being blind.

Sonora's story can be read in her 1961 book, "A Girl and Five Brave Horses". It was later made into a fictionalized movie of her life called "Wild Hearts Can't Be Broken", which was produced by Walt Disney Pictures.

The diving horses were a popular attraction at the Atlantic City pier before being discontinued in the 1970s after concerns from animal-rights activists (cited from: https://darlingmagazine.org/lady-legacy-sonora-webster-carver/)

Therese Renz

Born Therese Stark in Brussels Belgium in 1858, she was the daughter of two illustrious performers. Her mother was a circus equestrian, and her father a famed ringmaster. Her father left the family in her youth, and her mother, Lina, pined for her daughter to pursue a more stable life outside the circus, but Therese was determined to write her own destiny. At thirteen she left home to get extensive and elite training with the Wulff Circus in Switzerland. She made her official debut in April of 1873, at the age of fifteen.

Her acts incorporated extreme skill. A variation on high level dressage was the main event, what most people associate today with the Spanish Riding School in Austria: Levades, Courbettes, Croupades, and Caprioles. The horses would also perform the "Spanish Walk", various dancing and bowing tricks and, her most famous trick, jumping rope on horseback. Since women could not be members of illustrious riding schools or cavalries, it is likely that in the 19th century, Therese's life as a circus performer was the pinnacle of equestrian glory that a woman could achieve.

In the early 1900s, Therese's husband died, and money became harder to come by. Soon after, her mother took ill and died. Then in 1913, her son died young and tragically of a heart condition. With complete determination, Therese started her own traveling equestrian show in Belgium that included ponies, great danes, zebras, and even two elephants. Just as Therese was getting back into business, World War I disrupted her comeback and left her penniless. When the war ended in 1918, Therese was sixty years old, but that wasn't going to stop her. She joined a troupe in Vienna in 1923, and continued performing well into her seventies on a mare named "Last Rose", a fitting final partner. Therese died in 1938.
(cited from: https://www.horsenation.com/2016/06/02/horses-in-history-therese-renz-equine-circus-performer-extraordinaire/)

Dale Evans

Dale Evans (1912-2001) began performing at a very early age, singing gospel solos in church. Starting in 1931 she began singing with orchestras on radio programs.

In 1944, Herbert J. Yates, president of Republic Pictures, cast her in a leading role opposite Roy Rogers in "The Cowboy and the Senorita". Dale really didn't want to be in westerns. She had her heart set on appearing in musicals. Little did she know they would be musical westerns. Being from Texas, everyone assumed she could ride, but that was not the case. She learned to ride on the set, with help from Roy and the wranglers, eventually becoming a very good horsewoman! While waiting on horseback to enter the arena at a rodeo in Chicago, Roy proposed to Dale and then galloped into the arena before she could say no. They were married in a blizzard on New Year's Eve, 1947, at a friend's ranch in Oklahoma. Roy's wife Arline, had died of an embolism a week after Roy Rogers, Jr. was born in 1946. The marriage of Rogers and Evans proved to be a long and happy one.

Dale went on to appear in twenty eight Republic features with Roy, followed by one hundred episodes of the Roy Rogers Show on TV from 1951 to 1957 with her horse Buttermilk. Buttermilk was a young colt when he was rescued by a cattle farmer. He and other horses were on their way to the slaughter house. The farmer bought him from a horse trader. The horse had been severely abused and was very mean. The new owners quickly began to work with him and eventually he came around to become friendly and affectionate. These folks named him Taffy, and were training him to become a roping and cutting horse in competition. Buttermilk was called 'Soda' when Hollywood legendary trainer, Glenn Randall, bought him. Buttermilk was a Quarter Horse gelding. He was offered to Dale Evans because her movie horse Koko was too much to handle and he resembled Trigger too much. Dale fell in love with Soda and bought him. He was renamed after Dale saw a cloud pattern in the sky that reminded her of Hoagy Carmichael's song, "Ole Buttermilk Sky". Dale rode Buttermilk in almost all of Roy's movies and in all but six of The Roy Rogers Show TV episodes that aired from 1951-1957. A true Quarter Horse, Buttermilk displayed bursts of speed and could out run Trigger. On the set, Roy asked Dale to please hold Buttermilk back when riding along side of him; the Palomino they called "Trigger", always had to lead. Buttermilk died at age thirty one.

Dale was a very talented individual. She wrote many songs, including the couple's theme song, "Happy Trails". Other hit songs included, "Ah ha, San Antone" and "The Bible Tells me So". (cited from: http://www.happytrails.org/dale-evans.htm)

Tatiana Tchalabaeva

In the years before coming to Ringling Brothers Barnum and Bailey Circus, Tatiana Tchalabaeva was a gymnast and acrobat with the Russian National Team of Rhythmic Gymnasts. She then became an acrobat with the Moscow State circus where she met her husband, Kanat, a horse trainer. The Ringling circus became their home in 1991 until the closing of the circus in 2017.

Kanat and Tatiana Tchalabaev are originally from Kazakhsta. While performing with the circus, they lead an international troupe of riders (from Russia, Kyrgyzstan, Mexico and Uzbekistan) and created one of the most daring acts in the world. The five-person pyramid, "dead man drag", and underbelly climb are just a few of the precision feats in this enterprise. The troupe performed in a specially-designed forty six foot (diameter) ring on top of horses moving at galloping speeds of up to twenty five miles per hour.

With the Ringling show now closed, the Kanat Riders are performing solely with UniverSoul Circus. "We loved being with Ringling," says Kanat Tchalabaev, "and we love UniverSoul."

Tatiana and Kanat Tchalabaev live in Florida and continue to train horses and riders. (cited from: https://hobbylark.com/performing-arts/Life-After-Ringling-When-the-Circus-Closes-Down)

Camilla Naprous

Have you ever thought, when watching "Game of Thrones" or other shows and movies with horses, who trained those horses? Camilla Naprous takes care of some of the biggest stars on "Game of Thrones" — its horses. She joined the series during its first season for what was intended as a two-week job coordinating a jousting scene. That was almost nine years ago. As the show's horse master, she is responsible for coordinating and choreographing the many equine performers.

She and her brother Daniel run the Devil's Horsemen, a company based in Buckinghamshire, England, which provides horses to an array of film and TV projects including "Wonder Woman" and "The Crown." Their father, originally from France, fell in love with horses as a young man and once worked at the Lido, a Paris nightclub famed for its jousting horses. He eventually moved to England and, in the 1960s, started his own company.

Since they took over the business a decade ago, Naprous and her brother have taken the company to another level and "Game of Thrones" has been a large part of that expansion, providing unique opportunities to be bolder and more creative with their horses.

Camilla Naprous

But even relatively simple scenes require tremendous preparation. Just like actors, horses need to wear the right tack and often require makeup. Sometimes they need to look bloody or dirty or, as sometimes happens with stunts, one horse doubles for another. They also have different skill sets and personalities. There are horses trained to lie down, horses for pulling carriages and so on. "You need to be able to understand them," she says, "what they like, what they dislike, which situations you can put them in, who goes with what actors."

Her star horses include Tornado, a Hungarian warmblood gelding frequently ridden by Harington, and Dali, an Andalusian gray gelding ridden by Nikolaj Coster-Waldau, who plays Jaime Lannister, as well as Charles Dance (Tywin Lannister) and Sean Bean (Ned Stark). Over the years, the actors have formed bonds with their four-legged colleagues. "Kit and Nikolaj, they always ask about their horses and by their name," says Naprous. With pride, she notes that a horse has never been injured during the show's eight-season run. "If the day gets too long or the ground is not right or they need a lunch break, that's my job to stand up for them. They don't have a voice and I am the horses' voice." (cited from: https://www.latimes.com/entertainment/tv/la-et-st-game-of-thrones-horse-mistress-camilla-naprous-20190409-story.html)

Riders in the storm: Kit Harington, right, and Kristofer Hivju on their horses in a scene from Season 5 of "Game of Thrones."

In "Game of Thrones," the Dothraki are renowned for their skills with horses.

The Devil's Horsemen

Kit Harington in "Game of Thrones,"

In the Limelight

Limelight is an intense white light which is produced by heating a piece of lime in a flame of burning oxygen and hydrogen. It was widely used in 19th century theaters to illuminate the stage and was first used in a public theatre at Covent Garden in London in 1837. Actors who were the center of attention on stage were said to be "in the limelight". The figurative use, to people or things that were the center of attention outside the world of theatre, came into use around the turn of the 20th century.

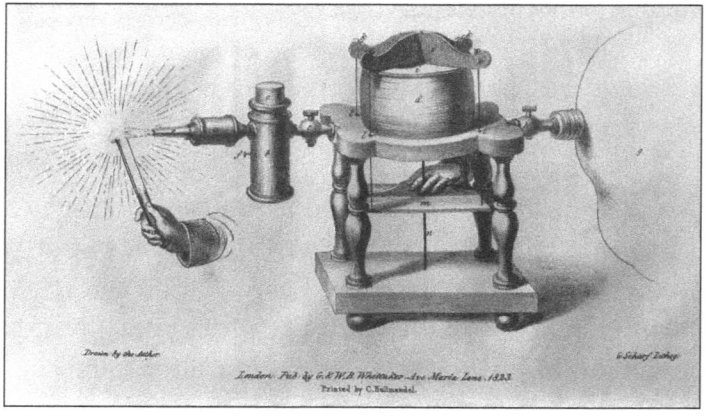

Thomas Drummond invented a practical Limelight, also called a Drummond light.

Any actor will tell you that it's hard to act with animals and children; animals and children tend to steal the limelight! Horses in particular are so big, that it is hard to ignore their presence! By the same token, it is also hard to ignore the presence of the person WITH the horse! There is just something about a horse that draws attention and puts you in the limelight - with your horse of course! Do you enjoy the attention you (and especially your horse!) receives any time someone sees a picture of your horse? or any time someone sees you with your horse? That's what drives a performer to perform; they love to be in the limelight and they love the accolades. They enjoy entertaining people and making them happy.

Are you a horse lover that fits the profile of someone who likes to be in the limelight?...shine on!

Check all boxes that apply. Then write down your favorite memory of performing with your horse or a memory you would like to create.

- ☐ *Do you enjoy receiving positive attention?*

- ☐ *Do you love it when people admire pictures of your horse?*

- ☐ *Do you relish the opportunity to take a victory pass at a horse show while the crowd is clapping?*

- ☐ *Do you like it when your horse makes someone happy?*

You're a performer!

_____
_____
_____
_____
_____
_____
_____
_____
_____
_____
_____
_____
_____

Competitors

Competing with horses is an excellent way to develop confidence, sportsmanship and a healthy sense of competition. It's also a great way to cultivate new and lasting friendships; hanging around with people who share your passion is always fun. Anyone who competes with horses will also tell you that it teaches humility and a sense of humor since things do not always go as planned!

Eleonor R. Sears

Eleonora Sears (1881-1968) is considered one of the leading all-round women athletes of the first half of the 20th century. Thomas Jefferson was her great-great-grandfather and her father was a shipping and real estate tycoon.

She was the first woman to ride astride at the National Horse Show, in 1915 and one of the first women to play polo against men in 1910. She won a quarter horse race in San Diego in 1912 and showed successfully at the National Horse Show for fifty years. She owned many champion hunters and was an early and consistent supporter of the USET (United States Equestrian Team). She also drove a four in hand and maintained a thoroughbred racing stable. She was elected to the U.S. Show Jumping Hall of Fame in 1992. She was also one of the first American women to drive an automobile and fly a plane! (cited from: http://boston1905.blogspot.com/2008/08/eleonora-randolph-sears.html)

Lis Hartel

In 1944, at age twenty three, Hartel (1921-2009) was paralyzed by polio. She gradually regained use of most of her muscles, although she remained paralyzed below the knees. Her arms and hands also were affected. Against medical advice, she continued to ride but needed help to get on and off the horses.

After three years of rehabilitation, she was able to compete in the Scandinavian riding championships. In 1952, she was chosen to represent Denmark in the Helsinki Olympics. Prior to this time, women were not permitted to compete in the Olympic Equestrian events. Even though she required help on and off her horse, Jubilee, she won the Olympic Silver Medal. Following her stunning performance, as Lis was helped down from her horse, a gentleman rushed to her side. It was the Gold medal winner, Henri Saint Cyr. He carried her to the victory platform for the medal presentation. It was one of the most emotional moments in Olympic history. She became the first woman ever to share an Olympic podium with men.

Lis Hartel is widely credited with inspiring the therapeutic riding schools that are now located throughout the world. Shortly after winning the Olympic medal, Lis and her therapist founded Europe's first Therapeutic Riding Center. This soon came to the attention of the medical community and Therapy Riding Centers spread throughout Europe. By the late 1960's equine riding was accepted by the America Medical Association as an "invaluable therapeutic tool". (cited from: http://www.equi-works.com/liz-hartel-therapeutic-riding-founder-passes/)

Sheila Varian

You can not talk about Arabian horse breeding in America and not mention Sheila Varian (1937-2016). She's an icon in the industry. In fact more than eighty percent of all Arabian horses in the U.S. carry Varian bloodlines. Her first defining moment came in San Francisco in 1961, when at twenty one years old, Sheila won the Cow Palace Grand National Horse Show with a mare named Ronteza. It was the first Arabian, the first female rider and the first amateur rider to win the Reined Cow Horse World Championships, a contest dominated by quarter horses. Amazingly, she bought Ronteza a for only seven hundred fifty dollars! She was inducted into the Cowgirl Hall of Fame in 2003.

The Varians were among the first to import Arabians from Poland. Varian said: "I didn't breed my stallions to follow any trends. I've always tried to take the best stallion and breed it to the best mare for the purposes I had in mind. I have had a deep fondness for the Arabians from Poland, however, I recognize that all Arabians came from the desert originally so quality is more important than origin." She had an individualized approach to training each horse; there were distinct attributes from every generation whether they were winners in Western, English or Halter Divisions. She inspired a new generation of trainers, owners and breeders. (cited from: https://www.horsetalk.co.nz/2016/03/08/arabian-horse-legend-sheila-varian-dies-79/)

Cheryl White

Cheryl White (1954-2019) was the first African American woman to be granted a jockey's license in the United States. Cheryl was one of the pioneering women who chased the dream to ride in professional pari-mutuel races during the 1960s and 70s. She began riding in 1971 at the age of seventeen. She won hundreds of races as a jockey. Cheryl finished her career in the Thoroughbred industry working as a steward's aide and patrol judge on the California racing circuit.

Julie Krone

Julieann Louise Krone, (1963-) is a retired American jockey. In 1993, she became the first female jockey to win the Triple Crown race aboard Colonial Affair. Krone became the first woman inducted into the Hall of Fame of the National Museum of Racing in August of 2000. She followed that in 2003 by becoming the first woman to win a Breeders' Cup race on the championship day, with Alain and Gerard Wertheimer's, Halfbridled, in the Breeders' Cup Juvenile Fillies. Krone retired from riding in early 2004 after winning three thousand seven hundred four races, while her mounts earned purses totaling more than ninety million dollars. Krone has been honored outside the Thoroughbred racing world as well. She is a member of the Cowgirl Hall of Fame in Fort Worth, Texas, the Michigan Sports Hall of Fame and the National Women's Hall of Fame in Seneca Falls, New York. She also received the 1993 ESPY Award as Female Athlete of the Year, the 2001 Wilma Rudolph Courage Award from the Women's Sports Foundation and the 2016 Amelia Earhart Pioneering Achievement Award. (cited from: https://www.racingmuseum.org/hall-of-fame/julie-krone)

Penny Chenery

Penny Chenery (1922-2017) was the owner of Secretariat, 1973 Triple Crown winner. She took over her father's Thoroughbred farm with little knowledge of horse racing. "Lucien Laurin trained and campaigned the horse, not me," Ms. Chenery noted long afterward in recalling Secretariat's glory years. "I discovered I had the ability to communicate with the public, though, and as the horse's spokeswoman I suppose people began to think of horses being owned by women." Laurin along with Secretariat's jockey, Ron Turcotte, and his groom, Eddie Sweat, shared portions of the spotlight with Ms. Chenery. But it was she who developed an uncanny bond with Secretariat. She holds the unofficial title of, "First Lady of Racing". She

was President of the Thoroughbred Owners & Breeders Association, 1976-1984 and she was racing's goodwill ambassador throughout the world. As a leading advocate and driving force for the welfare of retired thoroughbreds, she was instrumental in the formation of the Thoroughbred Retirement Fund. She was and Eclipse Award of Merit winner for a lifetime of outstanding achievement in thoroughbred racing. (cited from: https://www.nytimes.com/2017/09/17/sports/horse-racing/penny-chenery-dead.html)

Lucille Mulhall

Lucille Mulhall (1885-1940) is celebrated as the first cowgirl, an appellation bestowed by Teddy Roosevelt after seeing her ride at the Mulhall ranch. Legend has it that Roosevelt told her if she could rope a wolf, he would invite her to his inaugural parade. She came back three hours later dragging a dead wolf behind her. She was among the first women to compete in roping and riding events against men and earned such titles as, "Champion Lady Steer Roper of the World" at the Winnipeg Stampede and was often called Rodeo Queen, Queen of the Western Prairie and Queen of the Saddle. Lucille Mulhall's popularity was due to her skill, the result of perfect timing with her rope, unusual balance on her horse and her diminutive size and ladylike demeanor. Most important, she was authentic, coming from a genuine ranch background. She was inducted into the Rodeo Hall of Fame in 1975 and National Cowgirl Hall of Fame in 1977. (cited from: https://www.okhistory.org/publications/enc/entry.php?entry=MU006)

Tillie Baldwin

Anna Mathilda Winger (1888-1958) was born in Arendal, Norway. She immigrated to the United States at age fourteen and first trained as a hair dresser. She began her rodeo career riding during 1911 in Los Angeles, California, where she won the bronc riding competition. At the Pendleton Round-Up in Pendleton, Oregon, during 1912, she won both the trick riding and cowgirls' bronc riding contests. She was also a trick rider and relay racer. Later in life, she ran a riding academy.
(cited from: https://en.wikipedia.org/wiki/Tillie_Baldwin)

Melanie Smith

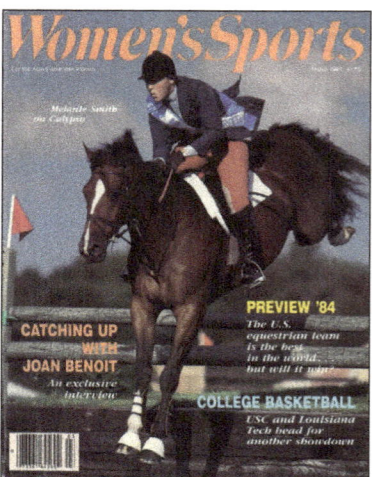

Melanie Smith Taylor (1949-) became one of only two riders to ever win the Triple Crown of Show Jumping: the American Invitational, the International Jumping Derby and the American Gold Cup—and the only person to win all three on the same horse, Calypso! After winning the World Cup Final in 1982, she was named the US Olympic Committee Sportswoman of the Year and inducted into the Tennessee Sports Hall of Fame. Two years later, she capped off her show-jumping career with a team gold medal in the Los Angeles Olympic Games. Melanie retired from active competition in 1987 and continues to serve the horse world as a clinician, a television broadcaster for major events (including the Olympics and World Championships) and a recognized judge for hunter/jumpers and hunter seat equitation. (cited from: http://melaniesmithtaylor.com/)

2015 Melanie Smith Taylor clinic

Helen Crabtree

Helen Crabtree (1915-2002) began riding at the age of four. By seven, she was showing horses for other people and by age eleven, she was training horses for a dollar a day. She became an American equitation coach in the discipline of saddle seat riding as well as a breeder and trainer of American Saddlebred horses. In 1970, she authored the book "Saddle Seat Equitation" which remains a primary guide for equitation riders. Crabtree Stables, which she ran with her husband Charles and son Redd, produced seventy five World Champion American Saddlebred horses and twenty two winners of the National Equitation Championships. She received the Lifetime Achievement Award from the American Horse Shows Association (now the United States Equestrian Federation) and was also the United Professional Horsemen's Association Instructor of the Year. At her passing, it was said that she helped make Shelby County, Kentucky the "Saddle Horse Capital" of the United States and "changed the face of the Saddlebred industry." (cited from: https://en.wikipedia.org/wiki/Helen_Crabtree)

Helen K. Crabtree Equitation Hall of Fame

Winners

Why do people compete? Is it to win? Maybe just to be around other people who share the same passion? No matter the reason, competition exists in every aspect of our lives. It's how you approach the competition that matters and horses are a wonderful way to learn how to be a good competitor! Competition forces you to give your best. Having a challenger right on your heels pushes you to be better, work harder and think deeper. You can also learn plenty from your successes and failures.

Women's instinctive nature to nurture, makes them formidable competitors! Women generally have an instinct to take care of things. Women tend to be more nurturing, while men are more competitive. When faced with an enormous creature who could do us some real damage, women feel the need to get to know and love it, thus ultimately gaining its protection, while men feel the need to master it, or somehow defeat it so it is no longer a threat. It's the nurturing ability of women that attributes to how successful women are as equestrian competitors.

Is competition all about the "win"? It depends on how you define "win". When we compete with others in a way that brings out the best in us and everyone involved - that's a win! When we challenge ourselves - that's a win! Did you make new friends? - that's a win! Did you learn something to make improvements for the next time? - that's a win! Every time you get on a horse, you're a winner!

Are you a horse lover that fits the profile of a competitor?....you're a winner!

Check all boxes that apply. Describe your last winning moment.

- ☐ *Do you enjoy a good challenge?*
- ☐ *Do you learn from your failures?*
- ☐ *Do you tend to nurture horses rather than feel you need to master the horse?*
- ☐ *Do you enjoy being with fellow horse owners at shows and cheering them on?*
- ☐ *Do you learn something new every time you ride?*

You're a Winner!

_____
_____
_____
_____
_____
_____
_____
_____
_____

Coaching and Carriage Driving Women

The World Coaching Club was founded in 1983 in response to men's refusal to allowing women into their club. Anne Wakfield-Leck (USA), Cordelia "Gay" Robinson (USA), and Cynthia Haydon (GB) started this unique club with Mrs. Robinson as their president. Additional early members were: Jean Lisiter Dupont, Margaret Ferguson Savilonis, Deirdre Pirie and Sidney Lenier Smith.

But women were driving four-in-hands long before 1983!

Cynthia Haydon

Coaches assembling for the Central Park parade, 1907. A clipping from an unnamed publication from the archives collection at the National Sporting Library and Museum.

The Ladies Four-in-Hand Driving Club

The Ladies' Four-in-Hand Driving Club was formed in New York City in 1901 by several prominent society women who took an interest in driving. The club was a counterpart to the city's famed Coaching Club, many members of which were husbands, fathers and brothers to the members of the Ladies' Club. The Ladies' Club took regular trips to the different boroughs as well as longer trips to destinations in New Jersey, Pennsylvania and Connecticut; for a short time they even ran a small shuttle service through Manhattan. Under the tutelage of renowned driving instructor Morris Howlett, most of the members became quite accomplished drivers. Each year, the Club held a parade and review through Central Park onto Fifth Avenue. The Club's founder and president was Helen Benedict Hastings, wife of the famous architect Thomas Hastings, designer of the New York Public Library, the front facade of the U. S. Capital Building and the Tomb of the Unknown Soldier at Arlington Cemetery. Other notable members of the Ladies' Club included Mrs. Arthur Iselin (vice president), Louisa Gulliver Sheldon (secretary and treasurer), Marion Hollins and Harriet Alexander. The Club flourished until automobile traffic on the city streets made coaching impossible. (cited from: Ladies Four-in-Hand Driving Club Scrapbook 1904-1910, Archives and Manuscript collections National Sporting Library, Middleburg, VA and https://middleburglife.com/then-there-such-hardy-perennials-the-ladies-four-in-hand-club/)

Mrs. Thomas Hastings, long serving president of the Ladies Four in Hand Club. A clipping from an unnamed publication from the archives of National Sporting Library and Museum.

Mrs. Thomas Hastings

Miss Mary Harriman

Coach of Mrs. Thomas Hastings, leaving the Colony Club in Manhattan, New York, Helen Benedict (Mrs. Thomas Hastings) with Eleanor Jay (Mrs. A. Iselin), and Florence B. Baker (Mrs. William Goadby Loew).

Ladies' 4-in-hand-club, Harriet Alexander driving between ca. 1910 and ca. 1915.

Photo by Brown Bros. from Town & Country, 1907. National Sporting Library and Museum.

Loula Long Combs

Loula Long Combs (1881-1971), daughter of lumber baron R.A. Long, was a world famous equestrienne and owner of Longview Farm in Lee's Summit, Missouri. She dedicated her life to raising and showing horses but she was well known throughout the community as a philanthropist and passionate animal lover. She drove high-stepping hackneys. In the show ring, she discarded the traditional side saddle and its habit of ankle length skirts to riding astride like her male peers. In 1967 Loula was elected to the Madison Square Garden Hall of Fame.

The honor was given to eighty eight outstanding competitors, two from every sport. She shared the equestrian honors with Major General Guy V. Henry, Chief of Cavalry, United States Army.

She ignored the accepted rule that women should ride in ladies classes only. She competed in, and won, open roadster classes that were usually for men because of the strength required to manage the horses. In London, England in 1910, she drove her prize winning horse, The King, as the only woman in the open roadster class, and won first place at the Olympia Horse Show. She won again in 1913 in Madison Square Garden where she shocked the more sedate Eastern men by racing her horse, Aspiration, in Midwestern style around the ring. Often turning corners on two wheels and flying past her competitors to the cheers of the

audience. Her showmanship gained her recognition from Barnum and Bailey who asked her to join the circus; a request she found amusing but declined.

Loula Long displayed her sense of equality in her personal life as well. As a wealthy young woman who traveled the horse show circuit at home and abroad, she was sought after by many with marriage proposals that she consistently refused. When a European nobleman traveled to Kansas City to ask for her hand, she took him to the stable to meet her horse, The King. The King expressed his displeasure by trying to nip him. Miss Long turned him down as well. Finally on April 22, 1917, when she was thirty six years old, she married Robert Pryor Combs, a man she had  known for years, the son of the minister of the Independence Boulevard Christian Church where her family attended services. Several years her junior, an age difference that was unusual at that time, she wrote in her autobiography, "My Revelation", that she decided to marry him when she observed him helping a team of mules haul a heavy wagon on a hill after being abused by their owner. (cited from: http://ridingaside.blogspot.com/2015/03/laura-long-combs.html)

Charley Parkhurst

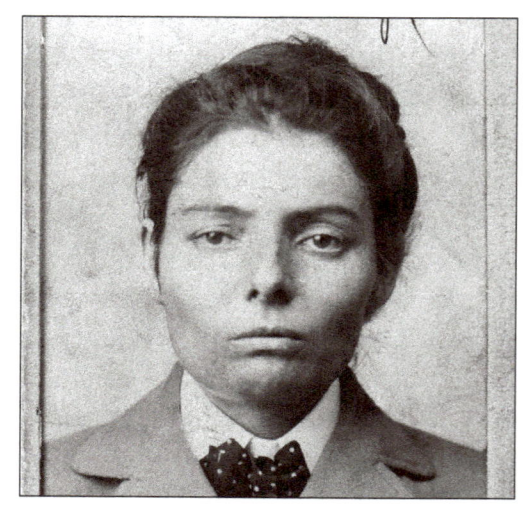

Charley Parkhurst (1812- 1879) was a legendary driver of six-horse stagecoaches during California's Gold Rush. She was considered the "best whip in California," by one account. Parkhurst had the makeup for it: "short and stocky," a whiskey drinker, cigar smoker and tobacco chewer who wore a black eye patch after being kicked in the left eye by a horse. Charlie had one other attribute, this one carefully hidden from the outside world. When Parkhurst died in 1879 at age sixty seven, near Watsonville, California, a doctor discovered that the famous stagecoach driver was a woman! Charley was Charlotte! She was considered one of the safest stagecoach drivers, not a daredevil, like so many of her contemporaries. She had a special rapport with the horses. She drove for Wells Fargo, at least once, moving a large cargo of gold across the country. Parkhurst could claim one other distinction: an 1867 registry in Santa Cruz County lists a Charles Darkey Parkhurst from New Hampshire as having registered to vote; more than 50 years before the 19th Amendment gave women the right to vote!

A. Sylvia Brocklebank

"A lady does not drive a four" but Miss Brocklebank of Great Britain did! The book "The Road and the Ring" is a lively account of driving in England from 1900 to World War I, based on her diaries and letters. The Nimrod Coach was built for her by Shanks of London.

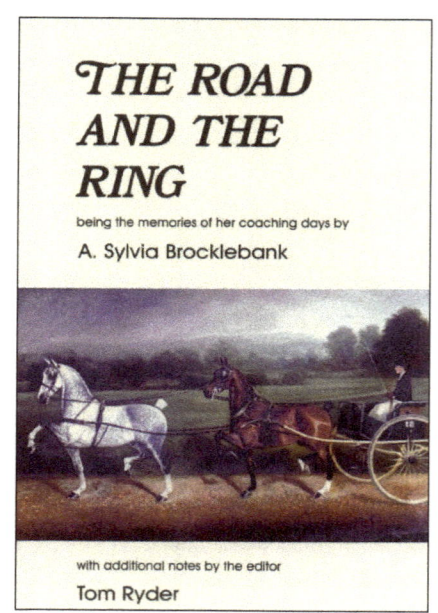

Alla Polzunova

In Russia during the 1990s, the interest in troikas declined to a point that even the existence of such a carriage and type of driving was under threat of disappearance. Thanks to a group of enthusiasts led by Alla Polzunova (1937 -), the greatest female troika racer during the Soviet era, the sport didn't die and is now making a comeback. The troika first appeared in the 18th century and was mainly used for postal services, for transporting passengers (mainly for long distances) and later in festivities such at weddings. The Russian troika is known for its high speed (up to fifty kilometers an hour/thirty one miles per hour) and was often compared to a flying bird.

The high speed was possible due to the special training and arrangement of the horses on the carriage. The horse in the middle, called the shaft horse, trots and acts like a locomotive, while the tracers - the horses on its sides – maintain a brisk gallop. This method of arranging the horses became popular not only for speed, but also for endurance, good cargo capacity, maneuverability and safety; a three-horse carriage was much more stable than the two-horse carriage widely used in Europe.

Alla received higher education at the Moscow Agricultural Academy and graduated in 1958 with a red diploma. Much of her early work is connected with the Central Moscow Hippodrome, where she worked as an assistant driver. At the age of thirty one, Alla obtained her trainers license. Busy work at the racetrack was successfully combined with scientific teaching and organizational activities. She engaged in postgraduate study with a prominent scientist, Mr. G. Karlsen, writing her thesis on training trotters. Since 1991, under her leadership, a specialized magazine "Trotting News", has been published, as well as an information site www.trotting.ru, which is very popular in fifty five countries.
(cited from: http://www.harnesslink.com/News/Alla-Polzunova-Celebrates-80th-Birthday-4-12-17-docx)

A Driving Force

Margaret Thatcher once said, "If you want something said, ask a man; if you want something done, ask a woman."

Women are "doers". You do not have to look far to see that women are the driving force behind so many things in businesses, communities, non-profits and much more.

When women were not allowed to participate with men, they did it any way.

Doers energize the people around them, making them enthusiastic to achieve their goals. Women are assertive in ways that are energizing. While being assertive women are able to exhibit friendliness, warmth, supportiveness and caring; all attributes necessary for successfully working with horses too!

Horses rely on good leaders; they are prey animals and rely on a strong leader to guide them and keep them safe. People who naturally have the ability to be a good leader work very well with horses while at the same time, horses can help people to become better leaders.

Are you a horse lover that fits the profile of a doer and a leader?....you a driving force!

Les Femmes Coche, Female Horse-Drawn Taxi Drivers in Paris during the 20th century.

Check all boxes that apply. What current projects are on your plate that reflect that driving force?

- ☐ *Are you a doer?*
- ☐ *Do you get things done in the face of adversity?*
- ☐ *Do you energize the people around you?*
- ☐ *Are you assertive yet flexible?*
- ☐ *Are you supportive and friendly?*
- ☐ *Do you set goals and are determined to achieve them?*
- ☐ *Are you a leader?*

You're a driving force!

_____
_____
_____
_____
_____
_____
_____

Authors and Artists

The short film "My Paintbrush Bites" by Joel Pincosy and Joe Egender tells the story about a horse named Metro Meteor, a retired rescued racehorse that nobody wanted who found a second career as an artist.

You may not be a professional author or artist but you are probably one at heart! How many horse books did you read growing up? Did you write stories about horses? Did you draw pictures of horses? Did you have only coloring books that had horses? If you did, you were (and probably still are) "horse crazy"!

Anna Sewell

Anna Sewell (1820 - 1878) wrote "Black Beauty" in 1877. It was her only published novel. The book made a lasting impression on Victorian Britain about animal welfare and directly led to the abolishment of the bearing rein. It is one of the most successful novels of all time and one of the most widely read books in the English language. It has been translated into over twenty languages with over four hundred editions printed. The book inspired three motion pictures and one television series. Anna Sewell portrayed the horse as feeling pain, just as humans, and brought awareness to animal cruelty.

Sewell's birthplace in Church Plain, Great Yarmouth has been the home to a museum and a tea shop. The house in Old Catton where she wrote Black Beauty is now known as Anna Sewell House.

Anna Sewell memorial fountain and horse trough outside the public library in Ansonia, Connecticut, in the United States of America. It was donated by Caroline Phelps Stokes, a philanthropist known for her work supporting animal welfare, in 1892.

Marguerite Henry

Marguerite Henry (1902 - 1997) was the beloved American children's author of fifty nine classic horse and animal books based on true stories. She won seven Newberry Awards. Her stories captured the hearts of generations of children and inspired many movies.

Misty was purchased from the Beebe's by Marguerite Henry when she was just a few days old. Misty's most famous trick was standing on her stool and shaking hands (just like Chincoteague Minnow).

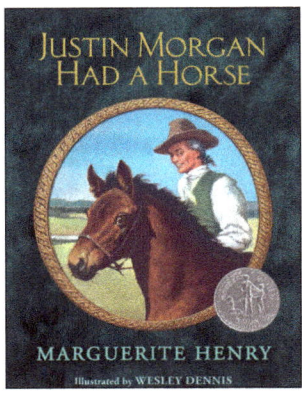

Marguerite Henry wrote the children's book Misty of Chincoteague in 1947 at Miss Molly's Inn there. Just up the street at the Island Roxy Movie Theater you can still see Misty's hoof prints in the front sidewalk. Misty actually attended the book's 1962 movie premiere.

Sallie Walrond

Sallie is a prolific writer on carriage driving, Sallie's "Encyclopedia of Carriage Driving", is a classic. She also offers many small picture booklets which are very helpful to the young and new driver. Her belief in the average horse person's ability to teach their horse to drive is a hallmark of her work.

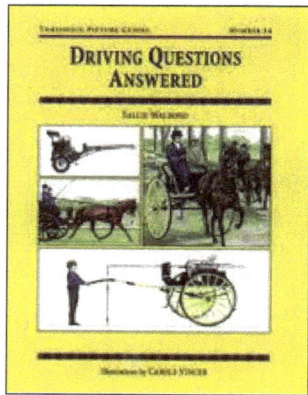

Sallie Walrond was born in London, England and grew up during WWII. She learned practical driving skills in the 1950's while working for a South London family. She joined the British Driving Society after it was formed in 1957 and become an Area commissioner.

Gloria Austin

Gloria Austin is a noted author of books about horses and history. She established the Gloria Austin Carriage Collection and is president of the Equine Heritage Institute, Incorporated, whose mission it is to educate, celebrate and preserve the history of the horse and its role in shaping world civilizations and changing lives. Gloria has successfully driven on four continents: Europe, North America, South American and Australia. She now lectures and writes about horses, carriages and driving.

Driving a Binder Beaufort Phaeton

 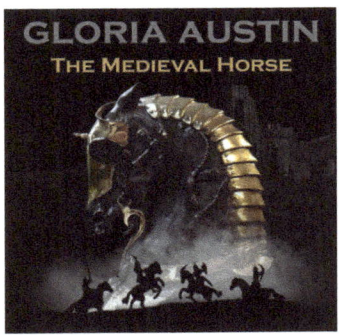

Coaching with PRE's at Walnut Hill

Jeanne Mellin Herrick

Jeanne Mellin Herrick's (1927 -2015) love of horses started at a very early age. She began riding with Margaret Cabell Self in New Canaan Connecticut and was part of her "Junior Cavalry of America". Jeanne's first pony was a little pinto pony named "Geometry". The next horse that came into Jeanne's life was a three-year-old grade Morgan mare named "Bonnie" who is ultimately responsible for Jeanne's lifelong love and devotion to the Morgan horse.

Jeanne began sketching and painting horses as a youngster and continued her studies at the Rhode Island School of Design, where she graduated with a degree in Fine Art. She went on to have a very successful career as a professional artist, author and illustrator. Jeanne's work is owned by some of the most important collectors of equine art in the U.S., Europe, and around the world. Her book, "The Complete Morgan Horse", is regarded as the definitive book on the breed.

On October 23, 1955 in Piermont, New Hampshire Jeanne married Fred Herrick, her husband of over fifty five years. Together they had a successful career breeding, training and showing Morgan horses. Over the years Jeanne was awarded numerous awards including the very first Morgan Horse Woman of the Year Award in 1964, as well as being inducted into the American Morgan Horse Association Hall of Fame in 1989, just to name a few. (cited from: https://www.saddlehorsereport.com/news/)obituary-jeanne-mellin-herrick-8123

Elizabeth Thompson (Lady Butler)

Despite never having seen a battle, Elizabeth Thompson, also known as Lady Butler (1846 - 1933), was a famous painter of military subjects during the Victorian era. One of her most famous works of 1881 is "Scotland Forever", which depicts a cavalry charge by the 2nd Dragoons of the Royal Scots Dragoon Guard at the Battle of Waterloo on all gray horses.

In 1874 she submitted a painting entitled "The Roll Call" (below) to the Royal Academy in London. The selection committee was impressed and decided to include it in the Academy's yearly exhibition. The painting caused a sensation and was purchased by Queen Victoria. The main reason why Elizabeth's painting created such a sensation was that she had taken a completely new approach to military paintings. Up until this time military paintings had shown panoramic views of battles or scenes of gallant officers performing heroic deeds. However, Elizabeth had painted a picture of a group of British soldiers after they had taken part in a battle during the Crimean War. Unlike previous military painters, Butler was interested in recording the pain and suffering of ordinary soldiers. It also caused a sensation because it was painted by a woman. In the nineteenth century there were few women artists. Those that did paint, did not paint military subjects. Eventually the public began to turn against Elizabeth's military paintings. During the first Boer War (1880-81) people in Britain became very patriotic. They now wanted pictures that glorified British victories. (cited from: https://spartacus-educational.com/Jbutler.htm)

Elyne Mitchell

Elyne Mitchell (1913-2002) was an Australian author noted for the Silver Brumby series of children's novels about wild horses that live far from humans in the secret valleys of the Snowy Mountains. These thirteen books – published in more than forty countries and many languages – take Australia to children around the world. The array of Silver Brumby web sites along with the movie and TV series of the same name, testify to their enduring appeal. The Silver Brumby, one of the success stories of Australian literature, never won a book award because, it was said, the judges didn't like the fact that the horses talked.

Her father, General Sir Harry Chauvel, became one of Australia's most famous soldiers after commanding the Desert Mounted Corps of thirty four thousand horsemen and camels in World War I. This was said to be the largest force of mounted troops since the time of Alexander the Great! The Battle of Beersheba, won by Chauvel's light-horsemen, has been called the last and greatest cavalry charge in history. When Harry Chauvel returned to Australia he taught his daughter to ride. She rode in the city and when the family settled in Melbourne's South Yarra, she galloped beside him on the beach at Point Lonsdale. Friends remember her as always being mad about horses.

Elyne Mitchell and Tom Mitchell

When she was twenty, she met Tom Mitchell, whose family had been among the first settlers along the Upper Murray. In 1935, Elyne married Tom. He was a champion skier, cattle farmer, lawyer and, later, the State Attorney-General. She moved to his cattle station in the foothills of the Snowy Mountains and fell utterly in love with her new home, describing it as "the land that built my heart." Three years later, Elyne had joined in Tom's enthusiasm for skiing and won the Canadian downhill skiing championships! Tom joined the Australian Imperial Force at the beginning of World War II. He was posted missing after the fall of Singapore and surfaced fifteen months later in Changi, where he saw out the war. Meanwhile, Elyne was alone in their vast home, built on a hill that overlooked the spot where the Swampy Plains and Indi rivers join to form the Murray River. So she wrote; a pastime she had engaged in since childhood. She told her daughter, Honor, that one must write something every day, never throwing anything away.

Elyne wrote until her final days, last sat on a horse (her palomino, Thowra, named after The Silver Brumby) three months before her death at age eighty eight, skied until age seventy seven, played tennis into her eighties and participated in the local annual cattle muster at age eighty five. At her funeral, the procession was led by Thowra himself. (cited from: http://oa.anu.edu.au/obituary/mitchell-sibyl-elyne-18137 and https://www.globetrotting.com.au/elyne-mitchell/)

Patricia Leitch

Patricia Leitch (1933 -2015) was born in Paisley, Renfrewshire, Scotland. She is best known for her series of children's books in the pony story genre about Jinny Manders and her wild, Arabian horse Shantih. The stories are set in the Scottish Highlands.

Her love of horses began when a friend persuaded her to go on a trekking holiday and she soon began writing about horses. She had many different jobs including library assistant, working at a riding school, a bookshop assistant, a primary school teacher and a typist, but writing is what she loved! Her vivid imagination is seen in her books because many of her books contain mystical themes with elements of Celtic and other folklore. (cited from: http://patricialeitch.ponymadbooklovers.co.uk/)

Lucy Kemp-Welch

Lucy Kemp-Welch (1869 -1958) was a British painter and teacher who specialized in painting working horses. She is best known for the paintings of horses in military service she produced during World War I and for her illustrations to the 1915 edition of Anna Sewell's Black Beauty.

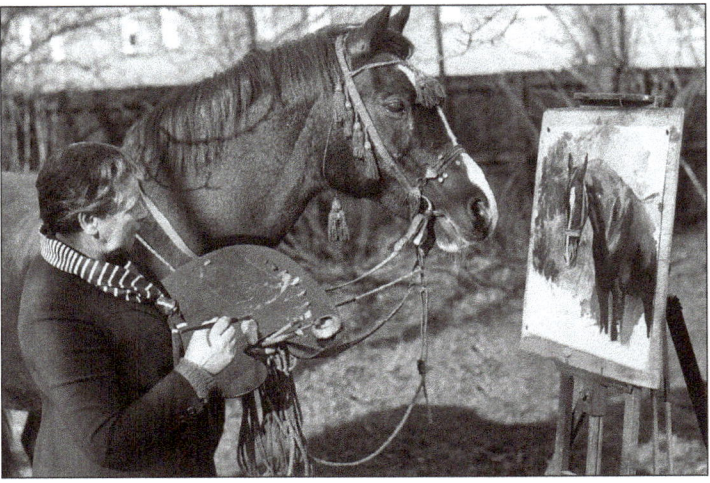

Belle Beach Bain

Belle Beach Bain (1875 – 1927) was a noted equestrienne, born into a prominent New England family who summered in Newport, Rhode Island at their cottage, Heartsease. Beach won numerous horse show ribbons, was well known as a teacher of riding and driving to women and children and was revered by horse people of her time. Beach originally published "Riding and Driving for Women" in 1912, and addressed such topics as form, mounting, and attire, and covered "the most important points gleaned in my career as a horse-lover and professional horsewoman." Over 100 photographs and drawings illustrate the book.

A quote from her book states:
"In these days of "advanced" ideas the advisability of women aping men in yet another way, by riding astride, is the subject of general discussion. Many "authorities" upon riding – "mere men", it is needless to say – speak with enthusiasm of the day when all women will ride in this, for most of them, ungainly and unbecoming fashion, Personally, I deplore this tendency and believe that it is a mere passing fad and that, except under peculiar conditions which I will mention, most women ride best and look best in the side-saddle.

The average woman is not built for cross-saddle riding; her legs from the knee up are too short; her thighs too thick; her hips too big, and she is cushioned too high to enable her to keep close down with the required firmness on the saddle. The side-saddle certainly insures a stronger seat, especially in the cases of pitching forward, as, for instance, with a stumbling horse or a kicking one, or on landing after the jump.

In riding, women are very generally accompanied by men, and there are few occasions when a woman has it in her power to look better – or worse – than when in the saddle. It is only those women who are built like men and very young girls who look at all well astride. A woman with merely a normally developed figure looks both ridiculous and immodest in this position, and in an English saddle thoroughly ill at ease."

Born in 1875, Miss Beach spent her life riding professionally and teaching the young ladies of society's elite to ride. A search of the New York Times pdf archives reveals pages and pages of articles mentioning Belle's exploits in the show ring and the details of her society life in New York and Newport. She died in 1927, destitute and suffering from cancer, rumored a suicide, having outlived the world she made her living at. (cited from: http://upon-a-white-horse.blogspot.com/2011/01/miss-belle-beach-let-time-not-forget.html)

Rosa Bonheur

Rosa Bonheur (March 16, 1822 – May 25, 1899) was a French painter and sculptor famed for the remarkable accuracy and detail of her pictures featuring animals. Bonheur was trained by her father, Raymond Bonheur, an art teacher. In 1836, three years after her mother's death, Bonheur met Nathalie Micas, who became a lifelong companion. By the time Bonheur was in her teens, her talent for sketching live animals had manifested itself. She rejected training as a seamstress and began studying animal motion and forms on farms, in stockyards, at animal markets, at horse fairs

Her visits to those public places, that were largely the domain of men, as well as her work in the studio, prompted her by at least the early 1850s to eschew traditional female clothing for the trousers and loose blouse of a male peasant. She continued to dress in masculine attire for the rest of her life, though she came to be mocked and disparaged for her garb. Like novelist George Sand, whom Bonheur admired, she obtained police authorization to dress as she did (1852).

She exhibited regularly at the Salon from 1841 to 1855, winning exemption from jury approval in 1853. Her work rapidly gained popularity in the United States and Britain. The Horse Fair (1853), considered by many to be her masterpiece, was acquired in 1887 for a record sum and became one of her most widely reproduced

works; The piece was donated to the Metropolitan Museum of Art in New York City. Bonheur's work sold so well that in 1860 she was able to purchase an estate with a château, at By, near Fontainebleau. She was the first woman to be awarded the Grand Cross of the Legion of Honour (1865).

In addition to animals, Bonheur was intrigued by the legends of the American West. When "Buffalo Bill" Cody took his Wild West show to Paris in 1889, Bonheur befriended him and sketched his encampment and its denizens, as well as painting his portrait on horseback. Micas, Bonheur's companion, died in 1889. That same year Bonheur met a young American painter, Anna Klumpke, with whom she corresponded for many years. Klumpke eventually traveled to France to paint Bonheur's portrait, and the two artists remained together at By until Bonheur's death. (cited from: https://www.britannica.com/biography/Rosa-Bonheur)

Leaving a Legacy

Leaving a legacy means putting a stamp on the future and making a contribution to future generations. Authors and artists leave a legacy through their works of art and their writing.

In our modern life, we've lost touch with horses. When it comes to the modern human-equine bond, out of sight really is out of mind. The Equine Heritage Institute was founded in an effort to bridge this knowledge gap. The Institute has a vast library of equine related books and also gives presentations and publishes books about horses.

Maybe you have not written books about horses or created equine works of art but in many ways YOU are probably leaving a legacy and bridging the knowledge gap. Do you share lots of pictures and information about horses on social media? If you do, you probably receive lots of "likes" and comments. In today's internet driven world, you are an "author".

Many legends and stories are not written down at all but are passed on from generation to generation. Do you have a horse picture on your computer and a co-worker shows interest so you fill them in on everything possible about horses? Do you talk about horses to everyone you know? Do you tell stories about equine experiences? Whenever you do any of these things you are storyteller!

Are you a horse lover that fits the profile of an author or artist?...you are leaving a legacy!

Check all boxes that apply. Share below how you are leaving a legacy and what drives you to share it.

- ☐ Do you share pictures of your horse on social media?

- ☐ Do you share information about horses on social media?

- ☐ Is a horse picture the wallpaper on your phone or computer that can be seen by your family, friends and random people?

- ☐ When someone asks about your horse pictures do you educate them in on all things horse related?

- ☐ Do you tell stories about your horse related experiences and adventures?

You are leaving a legacy!

Caregivers

Fred Rogers was famous for saying, "Look for the helpers. You will always find people who are helping."

Horses cannot speak. But, they do speak a language that some people can understand. These people are the caregivers.

Linda Tellington Jones

Linda developed a highly effective and revolutionary approach to working with animals. Her system of training, healing and communication allows people to relate to animals in a deeper, more compassionate way. Over four decades she has written eleven books, filmed countless videos and has over one thousand three hundred practitioners of her methods in twenty six countries. In 1992 she won a lifetime achievement award from the American Riding Instructors Association and in 1994 she received the honor of Horsewoman of the year for the North American Horseman's Association.

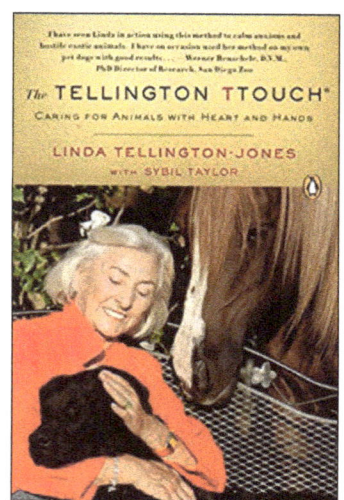

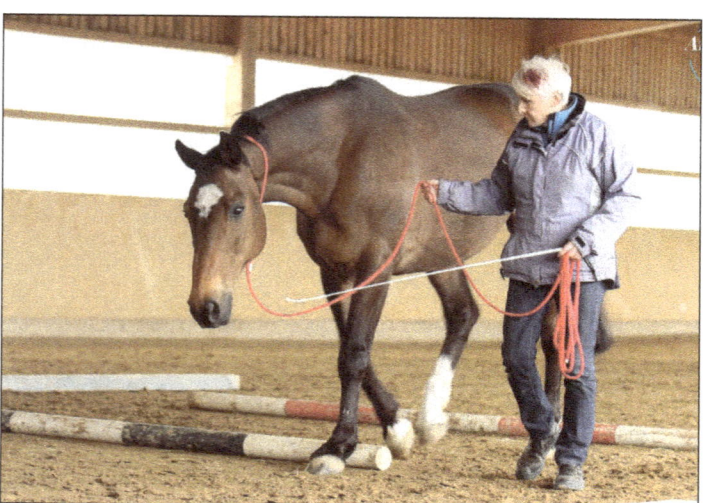

Florence Kimball, DVM

Dr. Kimball was the first woman to graduate with a degree in veterinary medicine. She was a native of Worcester, Massachusetts. Florence Kimball entered Cornell in the fall of 1907 and graduated with twenty one men three years later. She returned to Massachusetts and renovated a stable in Newtonville in which she opened a small animal hospital. Though relatively little is known about her practice, there is no reason to believe that it was not successful. In fact, in the January following her graduation, Dean Veranus Moore received a letter from Dr. Kimball indicating that her caseload was more than ample.

Dean Veranus Moore

Within a relatively short period of time, however, Dr. Kimball left veterinary medicine to enter the nursing profession. She trained at a hospital in the Boston area, may have served in the Army Nurses' Corps during World War I, and later worked at the State University Hospital in Oklahoma City, where she spent the remainder of her career. She died on her farm outside Oklahoma City in 1947. (cited from: https://animalpetdoctor.homestead.com/Historywomenvets.html)

Mary Ida Young

Like many significant achievements, Absorbine® grew out of humble beginnings—and through the tenacity of someone willing to question the status quo. In this case, it was a young woman in late 19th-century Massachusetts: Mary Ida Young (1865-1960). Her husband, Wilbur Fenelon Young, was an enterprising piano deliveryman who relied on the couple's team of horses to make deliveries throughout the Northeast. In those days, if a horse developed lameness, a common treatment was "blistering" the affected leg using one or more caustic agents. The blistered skin caused increased blood flow to the treated area, speeding recovery of the injury. Mary Ida knew there had to be a better, more humane way.

In addition to caring for their horses, Mary Ida was an avid gardener and herbologist. Through her knowledge of healing herbs, she formulated a special blend of herbs and essential oils into a tincture designed to increase blood flow and speed healing—without painful burning or blistering. Wilbur and Mary Ida started using her creation on their horses daily. They were so impressed with the results that they named it Absorbine® Veterinary Liniment, and Wilbur started carrying some on his deliveries. On one such trip to Syracuse, New York, he sold a whole case to trainers at a local race track. In a letter to Mary Ida mailed on his way home, he wrote: "I have had $42.80 worth of Absorbine orders this month. Let the good work go on. Some day we will make this boom … Lovingly Yours, Wilbur."

Wilbur was right. Everyone loved this humane yet effective way to relieve sore joints, tendons, ligaments, and muscles. Mary Ida had indeed invented a new treatment. They named their fledgling company W. F. Young — but it has always simply been called "Absorbine" by horse owners everywhere. The exact formula remains a family secret, but the results have been trusted by riders and trainers for more than a century. Mary Ida retained an active role in the company into the 20th century.
(cited from: https://absorbine.com/about-us/)

Carol Harris

Carol Harris (1923 -) is an American Quarter Horse Hall of Fame horsewoman and one of the first women American Quarter Horse Association's (AQHA) judges.

Carol made her mark as a famous breeder of Quarter Horses in Ocala, Florida. Her amazing horse, Rugged Lark, won the Superhorse award (a competition that includes western and English disciplines) at the American Quarter Horse Association World Championship Show in 1985 and 1987. He became the only Superhorse to sire two Superhorses, The Lark Ascending and Look Whos Larkin.

His legacy became top tier with the likes of Secretariat, Gem Twist and Big Ben; big enough to join the exclusive club of Breyer Horse models and be named America's official Quarter Horse Ambassador.

Ocala, FL Horse park arena will be named after Rugged Lark.

Rugged Lark died in 2004 and Harris created a memorial fund in Rugged Lark's name to benefit the AQHA's America's Horse Cares program. Money donated in Lark's memory helps create funding to support special needs children, individuals and organizations that benefit from equine experiences and therapeutic riding. (cited from: https://www.chronofhorse.com/article/carol-harris-and-rugged-lark%E2%80%94-bond-broke-boundaries)

Ruth "Bazy" Tankersley

Ruth McCormick "Bazy" Tankersley (1921 - 2013) was a wealthy heiress and conservation-minded philanthropist, and probably the world's most prolific Arabian horse breeder.

Bazy's father, Joseph Medill McCormick, owned daily newspapers in Illinois and served as a U.S. senator and her mother, Ruth Hanna McCormick, was an Illinois congresswoman. An early turn of fate pointed her Westward: Her father died when she was a toddler, and her mother remarried to a New Mexico congressman, Albert G. Simms. While she was growing up, and sometimes during breaks from schools back East, she honed her riding skills on family ranches in New Mexico, Wyoming and Colorado. By her early 20s, she already loved the desert.

Tankersley bought her first purebred Arabian horse when she was nineteen years old and opened Al-Marah Arabians in her early twenties when she and her husband moved to Tucson in 1941. Tankersley moved the ranch to Maryland in the 1950s but returned to Tucson in the mid-1970s. Over her career of seventy years she bred over two thousand eight hundred registered Arabians and was one of the largest importers of horses from the Crabbet Arabia Stud in England.

Tankersley also helped found horse breeder organizations, created a program to train young horse lovers and was a supporter of Therapeutic Riding of Tucson, known as TROT, a program that helps children with disabilities ride horses.

M. Phyllis Lose

At the age of nine, Phyllis convinced her parents to help her buy a horse and let her keep it in the garage. Of course, that was only after she rode her bike down to the local police station and asked if it was okay. At thirteen, her pony had outgrown its garage stall, and young Phyllis convinced her parents to let her rent an unused barn from a neighbor and make an income boarding horses, with great success. As she carefully saved her pennies, Phyllis was already hatching her plan to pursue her dream job as an equine vet. Lose noted that in 1953, the common belief was that "equine vets were on their way out," due to the rapid developments of city life and world changes. "They thought small animal practices would be where the money was," Lose said. But Lose knew from the start that she wanted to be an equine vet. When Phyllis graduated from the University of Pennsylvania veterinary school in 1957, good horse clients were not easily amassed by a female vet. She took on bizarre cases — like deodorizing a pet skunk or working as the on-call vet for the circus, and dangerous cases, like horses no other vet could approach — so that she could earn the trust of potential clients.

From her first paid operation to deodorize a pet skunk to becoming a world-famous "horse doctor", she has done more in her lifetime than many. Lose opened two equine veterinary hospitals in Pennsylvania and she was the first woman equine vet to do so. Her second hospital specialized in orthopedic, colic and soft tissue damage cases. It had an innovative surgical suite and recovery area. In addition to her private practice, Dr. Lose held many esteemed positions, including primary care vet to the Philadelphia Mounted Police and K-9 Unit, the largest equine unit in the country, and the track vet at Philadelphia Park.

M. Phyllis Lose, VMD, may no longer be practicing, but she is far from retired. She has written several books: "Blessed are the Broodmares" (1991); "Blessed are the Foals" (1987, 1998); and "Keep Your Horse Healthy" (1986). They have been translated into German, Spanish and Japanese. (cited from: https://www.veterinarypracticenews.com/first-woman-equine-veterinarian-reflects-on-her-career/ and https://www.horsenation.com/2013/03/20/horses-in-history-the-dr-m-phyllis-lose-story/)

Nurturing and Caring

Most human personality traits are unrelated to gender, but there are a few exceptions; in general, men tend to focus on personal goals and achievement (a personality trait called "agency") and women are more warm and nurturing (a trait called "communion"), and have higher levels of social intelligence.

According to writer Melissa Holbrook Pierson, in her book "Dark Horses & Black Beauties" horses are a lot like children; women know how to take care of children - it's in their genes. Women don't have anything to prove; they don't need to fix things in order to feel good. They're more patient, and horses respond best to patience." Women just naturally know how to nurture!

Most animals run from humans because humans are predators; our eyes are in the front of our head. Horses are prey so just imagine the trust a horse puts in a human "predator" to allow it near, to climb onto its back and lean across its neck in the same position a mountain lion would take to slash the animal's throat with its claws and jaws! A horse's temperament has to be divided into what is affected by nature (heredity and genes) and what is affected by nurture (the environment surrounding its life). Is it any wonder that the innate ability of a woman to nurture is what makes it so easy for women and horses to form a bond?

Check all boxes that apply. Write down how you nuture those around you? How do you nuture your horse? How do you nuture yourself?

- ☐ *Are you loyal?*
- ☐ *Are you dedicated?*
- ☐ *Are you confident?*
- ☐ *Are you a good sport?*
- ☐ *Are you responsible?*
- ☐ *Are you a trailblazer?*
- ☐ *Are you competitive?*
- ☐ *Are you patient?*
- ☐ *Are you nurturing?*
- ☐ *Are you a leader?*
- ☐ *Are you a dreamer?*

You're a horse lover!

An Amazing Woman

Write your name above and tell your story.

Sources

Deities
https://www.theoi.com/greek-mythology/greek-gods.html
https://www.ancient.eu/article/894/most-popular-gods--goddesses-of-ancient-china/
https://en.wikipedia.org/wiki/List_of_Celtic_deities
https://www.learnreligions.com/list-of-gods-and-goddesses-by-culture-118503
https://www.theoi.com/Ther/Hippoi.html
http://www.thaliatook.com/OGOD/aurora.php
https://www.theoi.com/Titan/Eos.html
http://godfinder.org/index.html?q=horse
https://www.learnreligions.com/rhiannon-horse-goddess-of-wales-2561707
https://www.rejectedprincesses.com/princesses/etain
https://www.maryjones.us/jce/etain.html
https://www.ancient.eu/article/153/epona/
https://www.themystica.com/astarte/
https://www.ancient-origins.net/myths-legends/aine-radiant-celtic-goddess-love-summer-and-sovereignty-007097
https://www.kamalkapoor.com/hindu-deities/ashwini-kumaras.asp
http://basquemythology.amaroa.com/personajes-mitologicos-de-vasconia/mari
https://mythology.net/norse/norse-gods/sol/
https://www.goddess-guide.com/sun-goddesses.html
https://feminismandreligion.com/2016/04/27/niamh-of-the-golden-hair-by-judith-shaw/
http://www.talesbeyondbelief.com/roman-gods/diana.htm
https://www.ancient-origins.net/myths-legends/dramatic-life-and-death-penthesilea-queen-amazons-002104
https://www.ancient-origins.net/myths-legends-europe/powerful-valkyries-icons-female-force-and-fear-003407
https://www.thespruce.com/snobs-not-allowed-1216906
https://www.psychologytoday.com/us/blog/hide-and-seek/201807/why-are-some-people-snobs
https://drhurd.com/2012/07/23/what-makes-a-snob/
https://horsenetwork.com/2015/01/10-different-types-horse-owners/

Warrior Women
https://allthatsinteresting.com/women-warriors
https://allthatsinteresting.com/zenobia
https://www.warhistoryonline.com/instant-articles/zenobia-queen-who-defied-rome.html
https://www.thoughtco.com/queen-zenobia-biography-3528385
http://howarddavidjohnson.com/legendary-women.htm
https://www.historic-uk.com/HistoryUK/HistoryofEngland/Boudica/
https://www.ancient-origins.net/history-famous-people/tomoe-gozen-fearsome-japanese-female-warrior-12th-century-002974
https://www.biography.com/military-figure/joan-of-arc
https://www.ancient-origins.net/history-famous-people/ten-powerful-and-fearsome-women-ancient-world-002947
http://www.silkroadfoundation.org/artl/sarmatian.shtml
https://www.ancient-origins.net/history-famous-people/lozen-intelligent-and-brave-apache-warrior-women-005889
https://www.horsenation.com/2015/02/09/the-first-women-warriors-on-horseback/
https://badassladiesofhistory.wordpress.com/2014/06/09/khutulun/
http://www.africaspeaks.com/reasoning/index.php?topic=1103.0;wap2
http://thefemalesoldier.com/blog/mai-bhago
https://www.nationalgeographic.com/news/2012/4/120419-female-gladiator-statue-topless-science-ancient-rome/
https://www.nationalgeographic.com/news/2012/4/120419-female-gladiator-statue-topless-science-ancient-rome/
https://www.ancient-origins.net/history-ancient-traditions/gladiatrix-female-fighters-offered-lewd-entertainment-ancient-rome-005272
https://www.keen.com/articles/spiritual/are-you-a-woman-warrior

Queens
https://baroquehorse.com.au/history-of-the-isabella-horse/
https://www.americanheritage.com/everything-you-need-know-about-columbus
https://www.vortexmag.net/en/the-strange-story-about-catherine-the-great-and-her-horse/
https://www.historyofroyalwomen.com/marie-henriette-of-austria-2/marie-henriette-of-austria-a-desperately-lonely-queen/
http://ridingaside.blogspot.com/2011/11/empress-elisabeth-of-austria.html
https://mrsdaffodildigresses.wordpress.com/tag/queen-marie-henriette-of-belgium/
https://www.elizabethi.org/contents/pastimes/
http://www.avictorian.com/royal_pets.html
https://www.historyextra.com/period/victorian/queen-victoria-death-funeral-mask-cause/
https://horsesandhistory.wordpress.com/tag/queen-victoria/
https://en.wikipedia.org/wiki/Elizabeth_II%27s_horses

Trendsetters and Reformers
https://www.wikihow.com/Be-a-Trendsetter
https://www.stylemyride.net/single-post/2015/08/31/History-of-Equestrian-Fashion-1920s-to-1940s
http://scandalouswoman.blogspot.com/2012/03/skittles-last-victorian-courtesan.html
http://wanthaveit.com/coco-chanel-and-revolution-of-equestrian-fashion/
https://www.crfashionbook.com/celebrity/g18874099l/elizabeth-tay-

lors-most-iconic-fashion-moments/
https://en.wikipedia.org/wiki/National_Velvet_(film)
https://fashion-history.lovetoknow.com/clothing-types-styles/equestrian-costume
https://www.epochs-of-fashion.com/fashion-icons-in-history/seymour-fleming-lady-worsley-and-military-fashion/
https://www.equilifeworld.com/lifestyle/horses-fashion-history/
https://www.horsetalk.co.nz/2014/10/06/sidesaddles-suffragettes-fight-ride-vote/

Performers
https://texashillcountry.com/saddles-grit-ostrich-feathers-life-of-prairie-rose-henderson/
https://nebraskahistory.pastperfectonline.com/byperson?keyword=Aspinwall%2C+Nan+Jeanne+%22Two-Gun%22%2C+1880-1964
https://centerofthewest.org/explore/buffalo-bill/research/annie-oakley/
https://darlingmagazine.org/lady-legacy-sonora-webster-carver/
https://www.latimes.com/archives/la-xpm-2003-sep-25-me-carver25-story.html
https://www.horsenation.com/2016/06/02/horses-in-history-therese-renz-equine-circus-performer-extraordinaire/
http://www.happytrails.org/dale-evans.htm
https://www.npr.org/sections/thetwo-way/2017/05/20/528778286/a-kingdom-on-wheels-the-hidden-world-that-made-the-circus-happen
https://hobbylark.com/performing-arts/Life-After-Ringling-When-the-Circus-Closes-Down
https://www.latimes.com/entertainment/tv/la-et-st-game-of-thrones-horse-mistress-camilla-naprous-20190409-story.html
https://www.phrases.org.uk/meanings/201400.html
https://blog.vet-advantage.com/equine/the-human-equine-bond

Competitors
https://www.localriding.com/competing-in-horse-shows.html
http://boston1905.blogspot.com/2008/08/eleanora-randolph-sears.html
http://www.equi-works.com/liz-hartel-therapeutic-riding-founder-passes/
https://www.platinumperformance.com/horses/horses-platinum-ambassadors-athletes/sheila-varian
https://www.nytimes.com/2017/09/17/sports/horse-racing/penny-chenery-dead.html
https://en.wikipedia.org/wiki/Tillie_Baldwin
https://www.okhistory.org/publications/enc/entry.php?entry=MU006
https://www.racingmuseum.org/hall-of-fame/julie-krone
http://melaniesmithtaylor.com/

Coaching and Carriage Driving Women
http://ridingaside.blogspot.com/2015/03/laura-long-combs.html
http://www.harnesslink.com/News/Alla-Polzunova-Celebrates-80th-Birthday-4-12-17-docx
https://russiapedia.rt.com/of-russian-origin/troika/

Authors and Artists
https://www.saddlehorsereport.com/news/)obituary-jeanne-mellin-herrick-8123
https://spartacus-educational.com/Jbutler.htm
http://oa.anu.edu.au/obituary/mitchell-sibyl-elyne-18137
https://www.globetrotting.com.au/elyne-mitchell/
http://patricialeitch.ponymadbooklovers.co.uk/
https://www.tate.org.uk/art/artists/lucy-kemp-welch-1397
http://upon-a-white-horse.blogspot.com/2011/01/miss-belle-beachlet-time-not-forget.html)
https://www.britannica.com/biography/Rosa-Bonheur

Caregivers
https://www.veterinarypracticenews.com/first-woman-equine-veterinarian-reflects-on-her-career/
https://animalpetdoctor.homestead.com/Historywomenvets.html)
https://absorbine.com/about-us/
https://www.equisearch.com/articles/as-young-as-you-feel
https://www.chronofhorse.com/article/carol-harris-and-rugged-lark%E2%80%94-bond-broke-boundaries
https://theblackstallion.com/web/tag/bazy-tankersley/page/2/
https://www.stridedressage.org/judy-downer-to-be-honored-at-usdf-annual-convention/
https://www.horsenation.com/2013/03/20/horses-in-history-the-dr-m-phyllis-lose-story/
https://www.theguardian.com/world/2001/mar/13/gender.uk

Women and the bond with horses
https://www.psychologytoday.com/us/blog/the-truisms-wellness/201607/no-horsing-around-about-the-human-equine-bond
http://theconversation.com/touch-forms-the-foundation-of-the-powerful-human-horse-relationship-95284
https://www.womenandhorses.com/denver_post050601.html
https://horsesandfoals.com/why-do-girls-like-horses/
https://www.horseloversmath.com/cowgirlsinhistorytimeline/
https://www.writingofriding.com/riding/why-ego-based-riding-fails/
https://www.horsetackco.com/horse-blog/what-3-characteristics-make-you-a-true-horseperson/